THE
RESILIENT
LIFE

THE
RESILIENT
LIFE

Manage Stress, Prevent Burnout,
& Strengthen Your
Mental *and* Physical Health

DR. SUSAN BIALI HAAS, M.D.

BEAUFORT
BOOKS

DISCLAIMER

This book should not be used as a substitute for medical advice from a qualified physician. The intent of this book is to provide general information in regard to the subject matter covered; it does not create a physician-patient, counselor-client, or coach-client relationship. If medical advice or other expert help is needed, the services of an appropriate medical or health-care professional should be sought. Coaching client names and other details of client circumstances have been changed to protect confidentiality. In some cases coaching client examples are a combination of details from one or more client situations, for the purposes of illustration.

CONTENTS

PART I

THE MIRACLE OF RESILIENCE

INTRODUCTION

I sat at my desk on a cold Saturday in January, engrossed in building a keynote presentation for an upcoming event. A parade of snowflakes floated by the window in front of my desk, spinning minutes into hours.

My phone shrilled, jolting my focus. It was a local number, so I answered it.

"This is the ski patrol calling. Is this Susan Haas?"

Everything froze. *No.*

I glanced at the clock: four thirty. The ski hill had been closed for an hour and a half. I'd assumed my husband was downstairs, relaxing in front of the fire. I was almost finished with my slides, and I had been looking forward to joining him.

"What happened?"

I struggled to stay calm, stopping myself from shouting my questions, as scenarios flashed through my mind. He had been in a near-catastrophic motorcycle accident on a racetrack a few years ago. A former ski instructor and self-confessed speed demon, he can't do anything halfway. We had debated this year whether his getting back into skiing was too risky.

"He's OK. He's a bit confused, but everything else checks out fine. We've put him in an ambulance, just to be safe. We're letting you know so you can meet him at the hospital."

Despite the encouraging report, anxiety engulfed me. As I drove to the hospital, I struggled to keep the car on the right side of the yellow line.

It's OK, I kept telling myself. *He'll be fine. In a few hours, after they've done the usual tests, I'll bring him back home. It's probably just a mild concussion.*

Once I got to the ER, I sent optimistic texts to friends and family as I passed the time in the waiting room. I asked them for prayers anyway.

After an hour or so, the ER doctor came and told me I could see him. I'll never forget the moment when the doctor put his hand on the handle of the door leading into the clinical part of the ER, then turned and looked at me intently.

"He's got cervical fractures," he said.

Never in my life have I been more stunned by someone's words.

My husband had fractured the two top vertebrae in his cervical spine, and two more in his thoracic spine. He could easily have died. Had he hit the snow at a slightly different angle, or if one of the people who got him down the mountain had made an error, he could have been completely paralyzed. Two of the fractures were unstable. One vertebra was so badly shattered that for months afterward his neurosurgeon wasn't sure that it would ever heal. And because of unusual features in the anatomy of his spine, he wasn't a good candidate for surgery.

"I'm sorry," was the first thing my husband said to me when I came to his side. He couldn't make eye contact unless I was almost directly above him, because he couldn't move his head. Trying to help him eat one of the cookies the nurse had brought, or help him drink some juice, suddenly carried profound risk. If a crumb fell down his throat and caused him to choke (which almost happened) or if it gave him a coughing fit, the results could be dire. It was all so surreal.

Incredibly, he wasn't showing any signs of neurologic damage. A CT scan, however, indicated that he had nicked a vertebral artery in his neck and was at risk of having a stroke. The next morning, they airlifted him to a larger hospital that had a team of neurosurgeons. It was terrifying, and I felt as if I were moving in slow motion.

The timing was terrible, too. This happened during one of the more intense periods of the COVID-19 pandemic. When it became evident that he would need to be urgently transferred to another hospital, my first thought was how I would get to him. The area we were in was surrounded by treacherous mountain passes, and a snowstorm was coming in. I was jokingly referred to by local friends and family as the "city girl," and I probably had about three hours of lifetime snow-driving experience. My husband's stepmother offered to drive me through the mountains to the other hospital, until something occurred to her. What if I wouldn't be allowed into the hospital to see him?

I called, and sure enough, no visitors. It was almost two weeks before I saw him again. We spent hours on the phone every day—thankfully I'd sent a charger along with him in a frantically packed suitcase. All he could do was lie on his back, staring at the ceiling, unable to move his head or torso. He never even saw the other patients in his hospital room; he couldn't see what was going on. He couldn't see his favorite foods (sushi!) that I sent him through meal-delivery services. The nurses would place the meal on the tray next to his bed. He couldn't turn his head, so he'd have to fumble blindly for it with an outstretched arm, bringing the food to his mouth and trying not to choke on it. He'd gotten a lot better at eating, but the thought of it all still made panic rise in my chest.

They eventually transferred him back to our local hospital. On the day that he came home, the hospital physiotherapist and occupational therapist spent a couple of hours training me on how to manage his neck and back braces. Days of preparations at home preceded this. There was over an inch of solid ice in front of our home, and it was too tricky to try to get him in through the garage with a walker. Much of our time before his return was spent worrying about how to get him from the car to our front door. We never anticipated that we might not even be able to get him into the car in the first place; that was a very hairy moment.

Family members picked up equipment from the Red Cross that would help him navigate our home. Because of pandemic restrictions, though, we couldn't have friends and family in our home to help. His mother could step in to help out of necessity if I had to leave the house, but that was it. We also weren't offered any nursing home support, probably because I was a doctor. I could manage the brace changes, and I knew how to watch for skin breakdown, infections, and anything else. Still, it was all so intense.

And then, a few weeks into all this, I fell while cross-country skiing. The time I spent exercising in the snowy woods had become my primary form of stress relief and mental health support. When I tried to pick up my scattered skis, I could tell that something bad had happened. The tears finally came. Over and over, I shouted, loud enough to awaken all the hibernating bears, "It's all just too much!"

Luckily I wasn't alone, as we were still allowed to exercise outside with others. My friends weren't fazed by my freak-out. They carried my equipment and walked me the considerable distance out of the ski park, encouraging and supporting me all the way.

When I walked in the house and announced "I think I've broken my hand," my husband thought I had to be joking. I wasn't.

Thankfully it wasn't a fracture, but I had torn a key ligament. I couldn't believe it when the surgeon told me that I needed surgery urgently in order to preserve the function of my hand. I said to him quite intensely, "You don't understand. My husband just broke his neck and back. I have a ton of virtual speaking engagements on top of that. I can't lose the use of my right hand. I have to be able to switch out his braces. I need to be able to do my hair. I need to be able to use

my mouse and laptop. I can't do this, not now."

He just stared back at me, saying nothing. He clearly didn't understand or empathize with the importance of my being able to style my hair before giving virtual presentations for large audiences around the world (and my panic at not being able to groom myself during a pandemic, when no one else could help me). Anyway, there wasn't any choice. It was surgery, or possibly losing proper functioning of my dominant hand forever.

As it turned out, I learned to do my hair and makeup (and pretty much everything else) using mostly my left hand, and I was even able to manage the neck and back braces one-handed. My husband and I innovated modifications that were better than our original techniques. We got through.

Shortly after, we took a rather hilarious family photo: me wearing my huge right-arm post-op brace (which I had to wear for 6 weeks); my husband in his neck and back braces (we liked to joke that he looked like a Stormtrooper); and our dog in her bright red "Superdog diaper," which she needed for bouts of incontinence. Shortly after that photo, she, too, needed emergency surgery. We had to laugh. The alternative just wasn't an option.

We kept repeating to each other that we were very lucky. He could easily have died or been paralyzed (and he ended up, miraculously, avoiding spinal surgery). His brain came through this huge accident completely unscathed. It only took six months for his spine to recover enough for him to return to normal activities, versus the two years that were originally anticipated (I have to say, a *lot* of people were praying for him). We live in a safe, peaceful country with universal health insurance. We were able to pay our bills. I didn't have to manage a bunch of kids or a newborn in the midst of all this. I'd always wanted children, but this was probably one of the few times I was glad that we didn't have any. All we had to do was get through a few very tough months. But it was still a gigantic test of our resilience.

We didn't pass this resilience test perfectly. These events really tested our relationship, on top of having had to live and work together 24/7, due to the pandemic. After we got past the survival phase of our accidents, it became clear that there were important areas of our relationship that we needed to work on. That work wasn't always pretty. It wasn't easy, and as I write this we are still working on various challenges. Still, without certain essential resilience factors that we were able to connect to, keeping us from drowning in despair and chaos, this season would have been much harder. In the next chapter, I'll share some of the key factors that helped us get through this hugely challenging time.

Many times, I shook my head at how naïve I'd been when I wrote my first book, *Live a Life You Love*, over a decade ago. In that book, I'd detailed how I rebuilt my life after experiencing severe depression and burnout in my ER residency (in Chapter 4, I'll share that story with you). From my late twenties onward, I'd devoted my life to helping others live more resilient, mentally healthy lives. It seems hilarious to me now, but by the time I wrote that first book, I really believed that I had completed, and successfully passed, my biggest life lessons.

In the years that followed, a series of unwelcome circumstances marched through my life. I'm weirdly thankful for these trials of life, including the two accidents and other difficulties that emerged during the pandemic. They exposed hidden weaknesses in my character and my life. They taught me to rely on and draw from the resources around me. They helped me develop a new brand of deep, determined resilience.

I'm no longer innocent enough to think that I'm done with life lessons. I can say, though, that with time and lots of practice, I've learned how to keep my head above water. I've learned how to keep myself from drowning in life's inevitable seasons of chaos.

According to Dr. Michael Ungar, PhD, author of *Change Your World: The Science of Resilience and the True Path to Success*, resilience only occurs when there is adversity.[1] Ungar, who holds the Canada Research Chair in Child, Family and Community Resilience, describes resilience as a process that all systems experience in adverse conditions. The phrase "personal recovery," for example, implies a change for the

better after experiencing severe difficulty. I love this perspective. Hold it closely if you, like me, have been through a series of distressing events in your life that seem unfair or hard to understand.

Since you picked up this book, there's a good chance that you're going through something difficult. As hard as it may be, there's a strong probability that it will strengthen you and make you better. Look forward to that. Remind yourself of it when you feel you can't keep going for one more day. And get help. Resilient people make use of the resources around them to get through challenging times and crises. Talk to your doctor about what's happening, or see a counselor. This book, as much as I hope that it helps you, isn't a substitute for either of these key supports.

Get a coach if you can, whether that's an executive coach, a life coach, or a health coach (depending on the type of support you need). Ask someone you admire to mentor you. Ask for, and be willing to receive, support from your community—for example, from your church or any other organization that exists to support you and your neighbors.

Resilience, simply stated, is the ability to recover from challenges quickly. The bouncing ball on the cover is intended to illustrate that. Life knocks you down, and you may hit the ground, but (hopefully) you'll recover, emerge stronger, and move forward. The odds are good that you will. Humans are resilient and frequently exhibit positive post-traumatic growth. Describing resilience as "bouncing back" doesn't quite do the process justice, though, and can create unrealistic expectations.

When life takes you down, it changes you. You're not the same after. We all can feel that—especially after living through the COVID-19 pandemic and all the other societal events, stresses, and shifts that happened at the same time. We've all been changed through these experiences. These events have impacted each of us in different ways, and we bear a variety of scars (and in some cases may still have active wounds). As we've adapted to all these challenges, we've emerged with new and different strengths as well. And some of us haven't "emerged" from it all yet, as there's still too much going on.

An article from the American Psychological Association illustrates this richer picture of resilience as "the process of adapting well in the face of adversity, trauma, tragedy, threats, or significant sources of stress."[2] "Adapting well" looks different in different circumstances and for different people. It's not as simple as just returning to a previous version of your life or self. The process of adapting can ultimately be positive and empowering, but sometimes it also involves significant loss. Regardless, it will always serve you well to meet your challenges in ways that support you best, and leverage the resources around you to help you adapt as best you can.

Resilience is something that you can learn, and build into your life. You can train yourself to be more resilient. I'll be talking about that a lot. It isn't all on you, though. Your ability to navigate the tough seasons of life depends on various factors in your broader context and environment. It can depend on the availability of, and access to, those resources and supports. It's important to understand these factors, which I'll get into in Chapter 1.

The "resilient life" is a way of being. It's a way of moving through life. It's a habitual, practiced, considered way of making choices. It's also a way of perceiving the things that have happened to you. It's an understanding of the factors—from physical and mental, to social, vocational, environmental, and spiritual—that work together to keep your head above the churning waters when they come.

And this is about more than just helping yourself be more resilient. In a recent groundbreaking review paper on toxic stress and aging, Dr. Elissa Epel, PhD, of the University of California San Francisco's Weill Institute for Neurosciences, states that there has been a paradigm shift in medicine, away from trying to cure unique diseases.[3] The new focus is slowing the biological process of aging. She gives the example that by slowing population aging, and thus decreasing the onset of dementia alone by just two years in individuals, one could reduce the number of Americans with dementia by 2.2 million.[3]

Epel references "social hallmarks of aging" that influence how

quickly we as a population age, including adverse life events, poor health behaviors, and poor mental health. Toxic stress ages us, as well—especially if we can't control it, don't know how to manage it, or don't know how to reduce its impact. This book is designed to help you counteract these aging factors by improving your ability to navigate adversity and stress, as well as increase positive behaviors, thoughts, and choices that can improve your physical and mental health. This may indeed help you slow your own aging process and reduce your risk of illness over your lifetime. The more people learn to live resilient lives (and are resourced and supported by society in living more resiliently), the healthier we all will be. We can age better, enjoy a better quality of life, and be less of a burden on our health care systems.

Epel also references two additional social hallmarks of aging: low socioeconomic status and minority status. Increasingly resilient people with improved longevity and health can in turn have more energy available to help address urgent societal issues such as economic inequality and racial injustice. This is truly a win-win for everyone.

Many books about resilience have been written by psychologists or psychiatrists. I'm a medical doctor, and I have frequently treated patients experiencing difficulties with mental health. I sought out some extra training in this area as part of my twenty years of general practice/primary care work. I also practiced virtual medical psychotherapy exclusively for close to a year, during the unprecedented mental health crisis of the COVID-19 pandemic. I had the privilege of counseling anxious, depressed, and traumatized patients from all walks of life, from both urban and rural areas.

Before medical school, I received my first degree in dietetics (nutrition). I love promoting and teaching wellness and preventive medicine. I've also coached leaders and professionals for over a decade, and speak to a wide range of organizations about stress reduction and burnout prevention. These various roles enable me to talk to you about resilience from a variety of angles and perspectives. I have also lived through pretty much everything that I teach.

If you start making even a fraction of the life-giving choices that I describe here, the challenges in your life will feel very different. The choices and disciplines may feel hard at first, but they *will* make your life easier over the long run. Everything, even the tough times, will feel better. In addition to helping us navigate life's great challenges, disappointments, and crises, resilience helps us rise above it all, flourishing and living with more meaning and joy.

I also want to emphasize that this book is meant to inspire you. My aim is to provide ideas, tools, and strategies that will improve how you—and your life—feel. If your life already feels heavy, it's not about piling on more weight. This isn't about more "shoulds" or more pressure. Read it from a light, curious perspective. Watch for ideas that make you go "Yes! I want that! I'm going to try that." I want to add *life* to your life. If you ever feel overwhelmed by the content, or how it makes you feel about your current circumstances, put the book down. Take a breath, step away, and go do something for yourself.

Life is a hard game. No one gets through it unscathed. Living with resilience isn't about escaping the challenges or building a bulletproof life. But when you make wise, well-informed choices on a regular basis, and are able to keep your head (and your center) when things get rough, you'll avoid a lot of grief. I wouldn't volunteer to go through some of the worst things I've experienced. Still, I'd much rather be this wiser, more resilient self than the more naïve, vulnerable person I used to be. Today, I make better choices. I'm more useful to other people and the world. You will be, too, especially if you can prevent life's tough times from taking you down. That, really, is the point of this book.

So, let's get to work.

YOUR RESILIENT LIFE WORKBOOK

I have a little gift for you, which you can use as a hard-copy or an electronic journal to go along with this book: a free copy of *The Resilient Life Workbook*. To get yours, go to susanbiali.com/resilientworkbook or scan the QR code on this page. I would suggest you go there right now to get it, so that you've got it ready to go as you continue to read.

The exercises in the workbook will help you go deeper with each chapter. You'll find "Coaching Exercises" scattered throughout this book. The workbook includes space for you to write your own comments (and action steps) in response to each of these tips. You'll also find additional reflective exercises. I'll ask you to think and write about a variety of perspectives, changes, and actions, as if I were coaching you directly. I'm excited just thinking about it! I hope you take advantage of this opportunity to apply the principles in this book directly to your life.

If the workbook isn't your thing, I encourage you to have a journal, notebook, or a similar note-taking device (electronic or paper-based), in which you can write down key points or insights that come to mind. Whatever you choose has to feel good and work for you.

You can also join me and my communities on Instagram, Facebook or Twitter by finding and following me (drsusanbiali). I'll share my latest thoughts and tips with you there, and would love to hear from you.

Here's to living more effectively and resiliently. It won't just make your life better—it will also increase your positive impact on everyone else that you encounter, both personally and professionally. Let's do this.

1

RESILIENCE AS A SCIENCE
AND A WAY OF LIFE

For most of my medical career, I worked as a primary care physician in urban walk-in clinics. Many of the patients would come to the clinic because their doctor was away, or because they couldn't get in to see them soon enough. Sometimes their words or faces revealed discouragement or hopelessness with their situation. Because of a diagnosis, or multiple diagnoses, they had resigned themselves to years of decline. I seized any opportunity I could to give them (evidence-based) hope. I loved seeing someone's face brighten with possibility.

Some people I met feared that they'd never be free of anxiety. They assumed they'd need lifelong medication, as that was the treatment they'd been given. Many patients with type 2 diabetes felt the same way. They dreaded awful, inevitable complications. They'd never heard that it was possible to reverse diabetes. Of course, potential reversibility doesn't mean that every single patient can be cured or will be free of symptoms or medication. Not every disease or every case is reversible. It can depend on the person's unique circumstances and the severity of their condition. Still, I wanted patients to at least consider that positive change might be *possible*. In many cases, the scientific evidence says so.

I've been studying and learning about the human body since I was a teenager. In ever-broadening areas of medicine, anatomy, and physiology, we've been discovering that our bodies (and brains) are capable of incredible change and healing. I'm more excited about these discoveries than probably any other aspect of medical research. We have proof of slowing and even reversing some of our most common diseases, and we have documented changes that scientists and doctors had once thought impossible.

Here are some of my favorite examples:

1. We can slow and potentially reverse "lifestyle damage" and aging at a DNA level.

In 2009, Dr. Elizabeth Blackburn, PhD, Dr. Carol Greider, PhD, and Dr. Jack Szostak, PhD, were awarded the Nobel Prize in Physiology or Medicine, for the discovery of how chromosomes are protected by telomeres and the enzyme telomerase.[1] Chromosomes are the threads of DNA that carry our genetic material. Telomeres are caps that cover the ends of chromosomes. The length of our telomeres points to our biological (vs. chronological) age and our health. Our telomeres naturally get shorter with time, but researchers know now that a variety of factors can impact the rate at which they shorten, and in turn the rate at which we physically age.

Four years after that Nobel Prize was awarded, I sat in the Joseph B. Martin Conference Center at Harvard Medical School, listening to the great Dr. Herbert Benson, MD. As I'll be discussing in Chapter 3, Dr. Benson is the Harvard cardiologist who discovered and characterized the "Relaxation Response" (RR),[2] our body's wired-in antidote to the fight-or-flight stress response. Sadly, Dr. Benson passed away earlier this year. I'm very grateful I got to attend a number of his lectures over the years, the last one in November 2021.

As part of a course on "The New Science of Resiliency and its Clinical Applications," via the Benson-Henry Institute (BHI) for Mind Body Medicine, Dr. Benson was speaking on "The Evidence-Based Emergent Self-Healing Capacities of the Relaxation Response."[3] He told us about a study he had just published,[4] in which he and his colleagues had demonstrated that people who were long-term practitioners of RR-inducing practices showed enhanced expression of the genes associated with the maintenance and protection of telomeres (read: slower aging, at a genetic level). In Chapter 3, I'll get into the details of the Relaxation Response, and its relevance to your life and health.

That same year, a group of scientists, led by another physician legend, Dr. Dean Ornish, MD, and including the Nobel laureate Dr. Elizabeth Blackburn, PhD, published the first study to show that changes in diet, exercise, stress management, and social support could produce longer telomeres.[5] This, too, could be described as literally aging backward. Since that early small study, other data has emerged, such as one study that showed that physical endurance training can increase telomere length.[6] According to a 2014 review paper, "there is now a robust body of research that suggests that there is a relationship between psychosocial, environmental, and behavioral factors and changes in telomere length."[7] I confess that I'm at the point where I'm starting to care a little too much about this aging process thing. I find this type of research to be more than a little comforting. It's also just amazing.

2. We can reverse heart disease.

A few years after I attended Dr. Herbert Benson's lecture, I sat in another conference room in Boston, this time at Harvard's Institute of Lifestyle Medicine's annual "Tools for Promoting Healthy Change" course. Dr. Ornish was lecturing, and I scrambled to write down everything. "Your body often has a remarkable capacity to begin healing itself," he told us, "if you give it a chance to do so."[8]

He shared the results from a classic Lifestyle Heart Trial study,[9] in which men and women with moderate to severe coronary heart disease were randomly assigned to either make intensive lifestyle changes, or receive what doctors would call "usual care," involving prescription medications and so on. A whopping 99 percent of patients who made lifestyle changes stopped or reversed their heart disease, based on cardiac PET scans that were taken five years later. Almost half of the "usual care" patients got worse and only 5 percent improved.

I've seen stunning images of arteries from similar patients, before their lifestyle intervention (massively clogged) and afterward (clear and healthy). The body really does have an incredible capacity for healing, and it responds to evidence-based, pro-health personal choices. That said, every case is unique. I'm not suggesting that you drop your medications and try to "heal" yourself. Please don't; not without discussing it with a medical professional. My emphasis is on what's possible, and how amazing—and forgiving—our bodies can be.

3. We can improve the structure and functionality of our brains.
When I first attended the "New Science of Resiliency" course, I learned about research and saw MRI images that transformed my understanding of the human brain and mental health. I had heard of neuroplasticity (the brain's ability to change and reorganize itself), but now I could see it with my own eyes.

One study, which examined the impact of an eight-week mindfulness program, reported that participation in MBSR (mindfulness-based stress reduction) "is associated with changes in gray matter concentration in brain regions involved in learning and memory processes, emotion regulation, self-referential processing, and perspective taking."[10] A few years later, a team that included some of the same researchers published a paper in *Frontiers of Human Neuroscience*, titled "Change in brainstem gray matter concentration following a mindfulness-based intervention is correlated with improvement in psychological well-being."[11]

I should point out here that research into the clinical and physical effects of mind-body medicine, particularly with respect to the popular (and often excessively hyped) topic of mindfulness, is still in the early stages. There has been criticism about the quality of studies and lack of clarity regarding the nature of interventions.[12] Dr. Benson himself, along with his BHI colleagues Dr. Michelle Dossett, MD, PhD, and Dr. Greg Fricchione, MD, acknowledged via a perspective piece on "A New Era for Mind-Body Medicine" in the *New England Journal of Medicine* in 2020 that "more robust, well-controlled prospective clinical trials are needed, as well as additional implementation and comparative effectiveness trials and basic research into the putative cellular underpinnings of mind–body health effects."[13]

That said, the current consensus, even among critics, is that changes in the brain do occur as a result of mind-body practices such as mindfulness meditation. After completing that course, I deeply enjoyed telling patients with anxiety, or those who struggled with negative beliefs and thought patterns, that they might be able to rewire and physically change their brains. Not just through mindfulness techniques, but also through traditional treatment approaches. Our brains are able to be remolded and are capable of change. Even if patients felt that their negative thought patterns had "always been that way," they didn't necessarily have to stay that way. That is such good news.

Your body and mind are magnificently resilient, even if your current state is the opposite of magnificent. Yes, you may have been through a lot already. You may not have taken the best care of yourself. And not everything can be fixed or reversed. But all is not lost. Your body—and your life—can be reshaped by fresh choices in remarkable ways.

WHOLE-LIFE RESILIENCE
Dr. Fricchione, professor of psychiatry at Harvard Medical School and director of the BHI, describes Resiliency Medicine as a combination of "stress buffering" and "health strengthening."[14] Increasing resiliency,

according to Fricchione, involves a mixed approach that includes leveraging the Relaxation Response; modifying thoughts and behaviors; cultivating positive psychology; maximizing social support; and supporting our minds and bodies through exercise, diet, and sleep. I share this whole life, body, and mind approach. Every one of these elements is explored in this book.

But there's still more to the full picture. Dr. Michael Ungar, PhD, and his co-researchers study the most difficult circumstances we can experience, from children who have been abused to communities impacted by large-scale disasters. One of Dr. Ungar's pet peeves is the overemphasis of the individual in discussions of resilience. He rightfully points out that there are elements of our environment that profoundly determine our ability to respond to adversity, no matter how much grit or wellness we may possess.

I started reading his previously mentioned book, *Change Your World*,[15] during that season of accidents and injuries. It was fascinating to observe, in real time, the truth of the twelve key resources that Ungar lays out, that "recur in resilient lives throughout the world." (I'll just touch on them here, using examples from my own story; I encourage you to read his book for a complete understanding of these concepts.)

1. Structure

"We all do better when the world around us provides structure and expectations," writes Ungar. Rather than resenting expectations that make demands on us, we should see them as a buffer against chaos in difficult times. Despite the chaos of the accidents, our dog still needed to go out five times a day. I had to take on all the household tasks (including my husband's care), and had that long list of virtual speeches that I'd been scheduled to give. It was stressful and exhausting, but it bred resilience. It got me out of bed every morning and brought out strength and determination that I didn't know I had. Be grateful for the tough-love demands of structure when times are tough on you. Remind yourself that these challenges are really good for you.

2. Consequences

Environments that hold us accountable build resilience. Negative consequences serve us over the long term, as we resolve to do better next time. Long ago, I canceled an important speech because of an extremely disruptive event that happened a couple of days prior. I thought about it a lot afterward, and discussed what had happened with wise mentors. Though it was understandable that I'd canceled the speech, the consensus was that it wasn't the right decision. In retrospect, I let people down, including myself, and vowed never to let that happen again.

In the intense days after my husband's accident, I considered canceling my upcoming speeches. Everyone would understand, given the nature of his injuries. But I didn't want to make the same mistake again. Some of the speeches were major keynotes, and large, un-reschedulable events would be significantly impacted. My husband also felt it was important for me to continue. I could do them all virtually, from home. It was the right decision. The consequences from that long-ago-canceled speech made me much more resilient and determined to persevere this time around. It felt good to dig deep and do what I had to do.

COACHING EXERCISE

Think of a time in your life when you handled a situation in a way that you now regret.

What happened? What was the decision you made, and what were the negative consequences?

When this type of difficult situation presents itself again in the future, how will you handle it differently? (Or have you done so already?)

How have those previously experienced consequences made you a more resilient person?

3. Intimate and sustaining relationships

I deeply appreciate the studies that demonstrate that just one loving, trustworthy adult in a child's life makes a substantial difference to the child's physical and mental health as an adult, even if that childhood was difficult and traumatic.[16] This illustrates just how important our closest relationships are to our ability to navigate adversity with resilience.

Even though we couldn't be together when he was in the hospital, my husband and I talked for hours every day. I would pray for him over the phone, sometimes several times a day. I prayed over all the tests, the decisions about surgery, his fears about frequent risky bed transfers (one mistake could result in paralysis), his ability to sleep… The list was long. We carried each other through those early days.

4. Lots of other relationships

Ungar offers wise advice: "If one wants to be strong during a crisis, it is best to invest in others before the crisis occurs." There's nothing like a disaster to make you appreciate friends and family. My mother-in-law became like an extra limb; she helped us with so many logistical things. My stepmother-in-law got in her car when she heard about the accident, driving more than two hours to be nearby just in case we needed her help. Church friends organized a "meal train," bringing us glorious home-cooked meals for two weeks. We couldn't have gotten through without people. In Chapter 7, I'll share more about the importance of relationships.

5. A powerful identity

When we feel respected and valued for our unique traits and abilities, we are more resilient. When it came to giving all those speeches in such a difficult season, the fact that those organizations valued me and really wanted (and even needed) me to help their people, motivated me to keep going and do the best that I could.

COACHING EXERCISE

What do you believe your role in this world is?

Who are you important to?

Lean into these aspects of your life. Let your value to the world (even if it's just your small corner of the world) sink into your bones.

6. A sense of control

I often talk about control in the context of burnout prevention. When workers are given the ability to make or influence key decisions that affect them, they are much less likely to burn out (I'll share more about this in the next chapter). Immediately after my husband's accident, I tried my best to minimize time away from my medical work. I didn't want to let down my patients or my workplace. Friends and mentors, who understood my personality, warned me that I shouldn't try to do it all.

Just as I was planning to get back to full speed with my patient schedule, I fell and needed the hand surgery. I could hardly type my patient chart notes, so I finally waved a white flag. The leaders of the mental health clinic that I was working at were incredibly supportive. They encouraged me to take whatever time I needed to recover from my operation, look after my hubby, and give all the speeches, leaving the timeline up to me. Having control over that decision made a world of difference. When your life gets hit by a crisis, identify what you do have control over. Make the best decisions that you can. And listen to wise people who know you well, when they try to give you advice.

7. A sense of belonging

During the season in which all of this happened, we had temporarily relocated to my husband's small hometown because of the pandemic. Though we hadn't been there that long, we had focused on building connections. As a result, when crisis hit we were surrounded by friendly neighbors, family, spiritual family, and a strong community. When you feel connected, you're much more likely to succeed in difficult circumstances. In these disconnected, hyper-digital times, it's more important than ever to nurture your connections.

8. Rights and responsibilities

I'm fortunate to live in a society that values and protects human rights, tries to learn from past mistakes, and continually works to improve understanding, truth, and justice in this area. Humans do best when we're responsible for ourselves and others. It helps a lot to be aware of this, as responsibilities can feel like the last thing we want or need when we're weathering a crisis.

In the early days after my husband first came home from the hospital, there were moments when I was tempted to just collapse. But I didn't, and I couldn't, because my husband couldn't shower without my help. His braces needed to be removed to change out the soaked pads, and this required him to roll, unsupported, onto his side. If not done perfectly, his spinal column could shift, the sharp shards of broken bone severing his nerves. Responsibilities keep us upright and moving forward in a crisis, when we may be tempted to avoid or hide from it all. I reminded myself of this frequently.

This doesn't mean, though, that you should try to do everything. Identify your responsibilities that matter most, and prioritize those. Give yourself permission to put aside things that aren't critical. You also need to evaluate your capacity to fulfill responsibilities without putting yourself and others at risk.

As I mentioned a moment ago, I took time away from my mental health clinical work during this difficult season. Part of the reason was that trying to "do it all" would put my own well-being at risk. I was also part of a large team of doctors who would be able to step in and make sure my patients got the support they needed. Given the extreme stress that I was experiencing after my husband's accident, I was concerned that I might be unable to provide the level of care that my patients deserved. Given my strengths and weaknesses when under duress, I knew that I would be more likely to be able to give a well-delivered keynote presentation under these difficult conditions than to provide the deep listening and support that my medical role required. I would also be more likely to make clinical errors. These factors added up to a responsibility that was best handed over to others, at the time.

9. Safety and support
My husband and I live in a very safe home and community; many people don't. This discussion of key elements of resilience doesn't pertain only to people as individuals; it also points to the work we all can and must do in the world, so that as many other people as possible experience safety and support.

10. Positive thinking
Dr. Fricchione included positive psychology in his list of approaches that increase resiliency. Later on, I'll discuss how to cultivate positive thought patterns as part of my strategy to fortify your mental health.

Dr. Ungar emphasizes that people who succeed have a positive future orientation that is grounded in a *realistic* assessment of their opportunities. I applaud this perspective, especially in the face of the societal idea that "you can do or be anything you put your mind to," and "if you can see it, you can be it." I confess that in what I now see as youthful zeal (aka ignorance), I used to espouse these ideas, using similar phrases in my first book and in my earliest inspirational speeches. I've since changed my song. Yes, life is full of wonderful surprises, and dreams can come true. But real life still comes with limitations.

My husband and I were intentionally optimistic about the fact that he would experience a smooth and full recovery, and we focused our attention on our blessings, big and small, every single day. We talked and dreamed about road trips we would take in the summer, if he were well-enough recovered by then. Still, we kept ourselves psychologically and spiritually prepared to face the challenges if things got tough. For months, the possibility of intense and risky spinal surgery was on the table.

I still encourage you to look forward to the good that your future surely holds for you. That said, a realistic embrace of what's possible (while still leaving room for life to delight and surprise) is a wise and healthy way to live.

COACHING EXERCISE

Is there an area of your life, or a specific problem, that you feel particularly negative about right now?

Write down some of your negative thoughts about this area or issue.

Now write down a list of realistic, positive thoughts that you could choose to focus on instead. What good can you anticipate, related to this, in your future?

---

11. Physical well-being

I'll be sharing lots of information on how to optimize your physical health. In addition to that, it's important to acknowledge that essentials like access to clean water and health care are huge factors in resilience that many people can't control or access. If you're blessed by living in a health-supporting environment, as I am, we can also turn our efforts to improving the environments of others who aren't so fortunate.

12. Financial well-being

In the days following my husband's accident, I felt the weight of the sobering financial possibilities. How long would he be off work? What if he didn't recover or ended up paralyzed, and couldn't work again? How long would I be away from my medical practice? I didn't get compensation for being away, and we weren't sure what kind of insurance he had through his work, or if he even qualified for it.

We had just bought a new home two months prior, so that increased the pressure. Thankfully, we had worked hard to pay off debts in the years prior to the pandemic, and we were in a better position than we had been previously. Of course, I'm aware of our privilege. I don't mean to cry "poor me"—that would be ridiculous. Still, investing in your financial health is a smart move that can make all the difference when crisis hits.

COACHING EXERCISE

What area of your finances needs the most attention right now?

What is one step you could take to start to improve this area? When will you do it?

Put a note or reminder in your calendar.

So there you have it. The wide range of concepts I've shared in this initial discussion form our concept of resilience, the foundation of this book. Next, I'll focus on taking the details of these concepts and turning them into more specific actions that you can take to transform and fortify your own life. As you become more resilient, you can use your newfound strength and energy to improve the resilience of your family, your workplace, your community, and your world.

In the words of Dr. John Denninger, MD, PhD, director of research at the Benson-Henry Institute: "There is no pill for making the world a less stressful place… Ultimately, finding ways to increase resiliency is necessary to combat the onslaught of the modern world."[17]

PART II

MANAGE YOUR STRESS AND AVOID BURNING OUT

2

REDUCE YOUR VULNERABILITY TO BURNOUT

I checked my watch. Ten more minutes until my presentation. People poured into the elegant conference room, and I was feeling nervous. I'd known this group of leaders would be mostly male, but so far there wasn't another woman in sight.

Despite the growing crowd, the room was strangely quiet. No laughter, no bantering. This was going to be tough.

I made my way to a back corner, near a set of open doors, and pretended to be busy with my phone.

"Dr. Biali!" An imperious voice, from my right, startled me.

I looked over and saw a bearded older man, seated in a solitary chair to the right of the doors.

"Yes?" I walked over to where he was sitting.

"I thought I should let you know that I won't be staying," he said, looking up at me with a smug expression. "I have a tee time in a few minutes, so don't be offended when I walk out."

I'd been asked to speak to this group about stress management and burnout; it was clear from his tone that he felt this was a waste of his time. His attitude caught me off guard, but I wasn't going to let him rattle me. I shook it off, thanked him for letting me know, and headed to the front to give the presentation. Once I got into the flow, time fell away as usual and I forgot about the unpleasant encounter.

The next morning I was in my hotel room, packing to fly home. When the phone rang, I assumed it was housekeeping or the front desk.

"Hi Dr. Susan," said a warm voice. "I hope I'm not disturbing you. I'm the guy who gave you a hard time by the back doors."

I almost dropped the phone.

"I'm at the airport," he continued. "I couldn't get on the plane without calling you. First of all, I'm so sorry that I was so rude. I don't know if you noticed, but I stayed and missed my golf game. The whole time, it was like you were speaking to me. For years, my family has been complaining that I've changed. They say I've become so negative and cynical. Secretly, I felt terrible about it, because they're right. But I didn't know what to do. I couldn't change the way I felt. But while I was listening to you, I realized that I'm severely burned out. I have been, for years. I finally know what's wrong with me. I can do something about this, I don't have to be this way anymore. It's amazing. Thank you. Thank you so much."

I had tears in my eyes by the time he finished. This story is why I do what I do.

BURNOUT: A SIGN OF THE TIMES

In 2019, an announcement from the World Health Organization (WHO) made news around the world.[1] A friend texted me immediately, when they saw the headline in their news feed. For the first time ever, the WHO gave burnout its own diagnostic code in their new ICD-11, the International Classification of Diseases. They detailed the basic three dimensions of this "occupational phenomenon" and briefly defined what it is and what it is not (which I will get into shortly). As a physician who has worked for years to increase the understanding of burnout in both health care and the greater business world, I literally jumped up and down when I got that text.

The word "burnout" gets thrown around a lot these days, but few people understand what the word actually means, what the specific symptoms are, and what one can do about it. It's essential to understand the basics of this syndrome, both to help you prevent it and to recognize it if it starts to rear its head. Burned-out people risk substantial negative consequences, including an increased risk of physical illnesses, sleep problems, conflict at home and at work, and developing addictions to substances.

Psychologist Dr. Herbert Freudenberger, PhD, was the first to use the term "burnout," back in the 1970s.[2] He noticed a pattern of symptoms in volunteer staff (including himself) who worked at a clinic serving people who were addicted to drugs. Initially, it was thought that burnout was unique to helping professions such as medicine, nursing, social work, and teaching. We now know that it can affect anyone who is impacted by a stressful working environment.

Given all the hype, I imagine you're wondering: How common is burnout, actually?

A study published in the *Mayo Clinic Proceedings* reported the prevalence of burnout in the US general working population at about 28 percent.[3] According to a 2015 report from Deloitte, as many as 77 percent of corporate professionals had experienced burnout in their current job.[4] Both reports were published before the coronavirus pandemic hit (and brought with it all the other challenges and crises that emerged at the same time).

Burnout increased so significantly during the pandemic that experts started calling it "the shadow pandemic." I had the opportunity to witness this firsthand, as I worked with dozens of organizations during this time. As part of my process of customizing presentations on resilience and burnout, I had the opportunity to talk with many leaders in human resources as well as members of various executive teams. I heard the same stories, concerns, and challenges, over and over, across different sectors and across the world.

Indeed, a job aggregator website surveyed 1,500 American workers in 2021 to determine levels of burnout in different groups.[5] They reported that 67 percent of people surveyed felt that burnout had worsened. Just over half (53 percent) of people working from home reported working more hours, and nearly one-third (31 percent) said that they were working "much more" than in pre-pandemic times. More than half (52 percent) of respondents were found to be actively experiencing burnout, with millennials the most impacted (59 percent). This reinforces the validity of a wildly viral *BuzzFeed* article from 2019, which described millennials as the "Burnout Generation."[6] The first generation ever to experience less wealth than their parents, millennials already had to deal with the new gig economy, paired with a continually changing and increasingly demanding work environment. And, as I've heard, their "old-school" bosses may not even believe that burnout is a real thing.

Unfortunately, women have also been disproportionately impacted by the pressures of the last few years. A 2021 report from McKinsey on "Women in the Workplace" found that burnout had increased year-over-year in working women, and that the gap in burnout between women and men had almost doubled.[7] As a result, one in three women had considered leaving the workforce or downshifting their career. Truly, the issue of burnout—and how to prevent it—has never been more important.

Health care workers have also experienced extraordinary pressure and trauma during this time. They, too, were struggling long before the pandemic hit. An editorial that appeared in the esteemed medical journal *The Lancet* in 2019 described physician burnout as a "global crisis."[8] We all know what happened next. The Physicians Foundation's "2021 Survey of America's Physicians" found that 61 percent of physicians reported often experiencing feelings of burnout, a significant increase from prior years.[9] One of the most heart-rending aspects of that report was that 46 percent of physicians had withdrawn or isolated themselves from others, and 34 percent felt hopeless or without a purpose. All this, while actively serving as incontrovertible heroes and heroines of our society. I've experienced burnout and despair a number of times in more than two decades in the medical field, in both severe and mild forms. I'll be sharing more about that later.

Any working person is at risk for burnout. Our hyperconnected-24/7 society, when combined with the unprecedented stresses of the last few years, has created an environment where people are more vulnerable than ever. The good news is that if you learn to understand the causes, recognize the signs, know your unique risks, and learn what to do about it, you'll be better equipped to navigate today's challenging work environments.

IS BURNOUT JUST BEING REALLY STRESSED?

We all experience stress, and stress isn't always a bad thing. Good stress even has a name: "eustress." This is the positive, stimulating, and even challenging stress in our lives that motivates us and makes us feel alive. We need a certain amount of stress and stimulation to function at our best.

In times of burnout or exhaustion, it's common to wish that you could win the lottery (or even get injured or sick) and never have to work again. When I was in residency, I longed to change places with hospital patients, so that someone would feed me and give me warm blankets while I lay in bed for days. Not a good sign!

Quitting your job might feel like a wonderful dream in the moment. The reality is, we do much better psychologically and physically when we're engaged in productive work of some kind. As a physician, I worked with many patients who sustained some type of workplace injury or disability. I knew how important it was for them (not just their employers), to get well and back to work as soon as possible. I remind myself of this, of how important working—or making a contribution to community or society—is for a human's well-being, on tough days when I wish my life could be one long vacation.

That said, when the stress in our lives regularly exceeds what we can handle, we can get into trouble. If that excess stress comes from work-related circumstances, it can set us on a course toward burnout. By definition, burnout results from work-related stress.

If there's no work stress, it's not burnout. While "stress" is a very general word, burnout is a syndrome with specific signs and symptoms.

I like this general definition of burnout, coined by a group of German researchers in an article in the journal *Burnout Research*: "An exhaustion of the organism which is caused by work stress."[10]

In their updated ICD-11 classification, the World Health Organization defines "burnout" as "a syndrome conceptualized as resulting from chronic workplace stress that has not been successfully managed."[1]I want to point out here, as well, that even though the WHO added burnout syndrome to its classification list of diseases, burnout is an occupational syndrome (a condition characterized by a cluster of related symptoms). It's not considered to be a disease or a full-fledged mental illness like major depression or generalized anxiety disorder.

It's noteworthy that the WHO describes the stress of burnout as that which "has not been successfully managed." Unfortunately, this sounds like it places responsibility for burnout on the shoulders of the individual.

Based on my experience and my review of the literature, and from listening to other experts on this topic, the burned-out worker isn't the first person we should blame. For sure, there are habits, choices, and thought patterns that worsen your ability to manage stress, like skipping out on sleep and working all the time. Still, workplace circumstances and culture are typically the primary drivers of burnout.

We see this in medicine all the time. Task forces on physician burnout point to root causes within the medical system. Doctors are known to be excessively self-sacrificing and are not very good at taking care of ourselves, but evidence suggests that we would still be holding up pretty well if we had more time with our patients, felt less pressure from administrators, spent more time helping people than staring at a computer, and weren't buried under piles of frustrating paperwork.

This book is primarily about helping *you* thrive and be more resilient. Part of that is helping you understand the context that you work and live in and the factors that play a role in your ability to manage whatever life sends your way. We need to encourage all people to be more resilient—that's what my work is all about. But if we don't look beyond the workers to the things that are wrong with the workplace and our work culture, we'll never turn this around. Maybe you, as you learn about burnout in these pages, might even contribute to that change that many workplaces so desperately need.

SO HOW DO YOU KNOW IF YOU'RE BURNED OUT?

In its ICD-11 description, the WHO defined three dimensions that characterize burnout. Most experts agree on these three key clinical criteria (first described by Maslach and Jackson in 1981[11]): feelings of energy depletion or exhaustion; increased mental distance from one's job, with feelings of negativism or cynicism related to one's job; and reduced professional efficacy.[1]

1. Emotional exhaustion

You wake up every morning, not knowing how you'll face the day. Tasks that used to feel simple or routine now feel overwhelming. Your tank is empty, and a weekend off (or a week off) won't fill it back up.

Before I say anything else, I must point out that there are other things that can cause you to feel this way. For example, depression and burnout can present with similar symptoms, so it's important not to diagnose yourself (the information in this book should never replace getting help and personalized medical advice from your physician). Physical conditions such as an underactive thyroid or low iron levels can cause similar exhaustion. If you're feeling unusually awful, exhausted, or down, be sure to see your doctor first.

On a side note, some experts believe that burnout is actually a form of depression and not a distinct syndrome or condition of its own.[12] This is a point of controversy in the field, but I fall into the camp that believes that burnout is a distinct condition.

Some studies have reported a shared overlap between depression and burnout,[13] and the two conditions are more likely to coexist in someone who is severely burned out. That's what happened to me. I was diagnosed with severe depression during my ER residency training, but I appreciate now that burnout played just as much or even more of a role in the symptoms that I was experiencing.

2. Depersonalization and cynicism

In the medical clinic setting where I worked for a couple of decades, the first sign that I may have been teetering toward burnout was my irritation with patients. I'd start to feel impatient if someone was taking too long to explain their situation. I'd resent when someone insisted that they needed to be squeezed in to see me (for urgent, legitimate reasons), at the end of a long day. My compassion for people palpably dwindled. A numb sense of trying to just get through the day would take its place.

Some doctors have felt this way for years, similar to the man I met in the opening of this chapter. You have probably met some of these doctors! I've heard terrible stories about callous, brusque physicians. Some people are mean or unkind. But most of those "awful" doctors were probably burned out. The same goes for any grumpy, negative person-on-the-job that you may encounter anywhere.

When you experience the depersonalization of burnout, you stop seeing people as people. It's as if your brain turns off your compassion, your ability to identify with others and their problems and concerns, as a self-protective mechanism. You become noticeably cynical. You might start using a critical or mocking tone when talking about people who make demands on you at work. You may even start treating people badly. This impacts your relationships with both clients and coworkers, creating a spiral of negativity.

I often say that others might notice this shift in your personality before you do. They may joke about it, or complain about it. You might also notice yourself complaining more about your work or organization. You feel resentful or unusually negative about your work environment and tasks.

Cultivate more compassion for yourself, and others, if you observe this phenomenon. If you've become markedly more negative, don't judge yourself harshly. See it as a red flag pointing to something very important. You could be burning out, and all this negativity may simply be your brain crying for help. Don't ignore it.

3. Reduced personal accomplishment or efficacy

When you're worn out from work-related stress, you don't perform at your best. It's no surprise that burned-out people feel anxious about the quality of their performance, and start to lose their confidence. Maslach and Jackson describe this third hallmark of burnout: "Workers feel unhappy about themselves and dissatisfied with their accomplishments on the job."[11] If you used to feel confident about your work but now find yourself doubting your abilities or feeling unfit for your job, that could be burnout talking—especially if you enjoyed your work in the past and felt like it was the right place for you to be.

I also caution people to be careful about quitting when you feel like this. Burnout feels awful, and the desire to quit can be really tempting. Sometimes that's the right decision. In my experience as a coach, though, I've seen that if negative organizational or team dynamics get addressed, and you learn better boundaries and take better care of yourself, things typically feel much better and your appreciation for your work returns.

WORKPLACE FACTORS: IT'S NOT JUST HEAVY WORKLOADS

I really want to help you avoid burnout. In order to give you the best shot, let's explore different factors that make you vulnerable. We'll start by looking at the risks you may face in your workplace.

Leiter and Maslach were the first to identify six "areas of worklife" that span the major organizational precursors to burnout.[14] Their findings in these areas inform each of the sections that I've listed below. Ultimately, each area of worklife impacts the ways in which people and the organizations that they work for establish—or fail to establish—a positive, enduring working relationship.

Most of my coaching clients are leaders in some capacity. There's a good possibility that you are, too, in which case this isn't just about your experience as an employee. As a leader, it's essential to understand how these different factors either protect or threaten the well-being and engagement of your people. Organizational leaders must seek to understand and examine these factors, as well, and take real steps to reduce the pressures that lead to burnout in their employees.

1. Heavy workloads

Not surprisingly, studies have consistently connected heavy (or increasing) workloads to burnout. People who don't have time or opportunity to fully recover from intense, demanding work periods are at high risk for becoming chronically exhausted.

Here's something you might not be aware of, though: If your work requires you to display emotions that you aren't actually feeling (such as pretending you're cheery and happy when you're actually exhausted or miserable), it makes your work much more draining. I had to do this all the time while practicing medicine. In a given day, all kinds of things would happen that would negatively impact my emotions. I may have had to tell someone that they had cancer. I may have had to deal with a particularly demanding or verbally abusive individual. I could be running an hour behind because of things beyond my control, feeling extremely stressed by the pressure of a packed waiting room. Yet no matter what was going on, I felt that when I opened the examining room door to see the next patient, I had to greet them with a cheerful hello and a smile, and give them my full attention. I'd learned early on that if I didn't don this mask, things would get worse. People who have been waiting forever to see a doctor are often irritable and annoyed. They're not ready to cut you much slack, and not very interested in the kind of day you're having. Better to just hide it altogether. I see now that I should have left more room for my real self in this equation.

Here are some tips to help you offset high workloads.

- **Don't take on work that isn't yours.** I see this all the time, especially in leaders. You may not even realize how often you're doing this. Some things may get done better and faster if you do them, which is why you keep taking them over. But when you take on the work of others, you deprive those individuals of opportunities to learn and grow. You also deprive yourself of time and energy that you need for what you alone can do (and need to do). In Chapter 8, I'll give you some suggestions for how to shift this habit.

- **Tackle your hardest task early in the day.** Planning and prioritizing your work is key to managing a high workload. If there's something you're dreading or tempted to procrastinate about, get it out of the way as soon as you can. Make a habit of doing the hardest or most unappealing task early in your day, and the rest of your day will feel much lighter. This is so much better than the oppressive, nagging feeling that weighs you down when you keep putting something off.

- **Make the most of any opportunities to take a break.** Take your coffee breaks, and get away from your desk whenever you can (get some water, stretch your legs, take a real lunch break, etc.).

- **If you can't do it all, ask your supervisor what to prioritize.** I often hear of organizations in which new "priorities" get piled on top of existing priorities. How can they all be priorities? If it's impossible to do everything that's on your plate, consider asking your manager what they would suggest you focus on as a true priority.

- **Use all your vacation time.** This discipline provides the rest you need to recover and recharge, and will make you more productive when you return. If you're hesitant to take desperately needed time off, remind yourself of this: taking your vacation time can actually increase the probability that you'll get a raise or a promotion.[15] You don't need to go anywhere, either. I've come to really enjoy staycations with good boundaries (being careful to stay away from anything work-related). I appreciate a restful, hassle-free vacation at home that involves little-to-no planning, packing, traveling, or extra spending! You may also be able to use your vacation days to take extra days off here and there. One of the leaders I work with, whose work makes it really hard to take chunks of time away, found that using individual vacation days to create long weekends helps a lot.

- **Honor your emotions.** If your work requires you to be "on" all the time, no matter how you feel, make sure you give yourself opportunities to process your true feelings. Be real with friends and family and receive their support. Seek counseling if you're feeling unusually stressed or upset. Journal about your day in the evening, to process and acknowledge how things really went or felt.

- **Drop the perfectionism.** If you're drowning in a heavy workload, you might have to lower your standards in order to survive. One of my executive clients, who has extremely high standards, practices producing results that are merely "adequate" (for projects of lesser importance, for example). They're a perfectionist, so even the word "adequate" drives them crazy, but this is an essential skill if they want to accomplish all they're tasked to do. The same goes for work that requires you to present a façade. I didn't need to be such a cheery doctor; it would have been less draining and more sustainable as a job if I had been just quietly nice to people.

2. Lack of control

According to Leiter and Maslach: "Autonomy is consistent with personal accomplishment and incompatible with exhaustion."[14] Being micro-managed puts you at risk for burnout (if you're a leader, be aware of this with your people). Experiencing uncontrollable changes to your job will increase your stress level, as well. This happened to many during the pandemic. Overnight, millions found themselves working from home, while others had to adapt to new workplace protocols designed to keep everyone safe.

In these stressful, uncertain, and frequently changing circumstances, leaders constantly asked me how they could best support their people. I encouraged them to look for ways to give people control of anything that they could. That might be through a more flexible schedule, or more agency in how team members approach or prioritize their work. I also regularly told employees to think about what they really need, to identify what would help them feel better and in more control, and to ask for it. You'd be surprised by how many ways we can improve our own circumstances if we just ask. And there are lots of ways that we might help others if we have influence.

You may also experience lack of control through "role conflict." This can arise if you prefer to focus your time on certain tasks or areas but are asked to do other things instead. It can also happen if you're faced with contradictory demands. If you're a manager, your supervisor might ask you to do something or go in a direction that conflicts with what your team members hope for or need. Circumstances like these can feel paralyzing, frustrating, and extremely stressful.

One of my clients, a manager in a leading multinational corporation, has been dealing with severe role conflict in the past year. Highly skilled and experienced in certain areas, she longs to bring her best to her job. She felt deeply frustrated, watching from the sidelines as plum projects that she would love were handed out to others. In several cases, they were less qualified than she was. She fantasized regularly about quitting.

Lately she's been trying a new tack. She started organizing one-on-one lunch or coffee meetings with influential leaders in the organization, to discuss her ideas and areas of interest, and to make them more aware of her wealth of experience and strengths. As a result, she has recently been moved to a more relevant area in the organization and is excited by the possibility of making a stronger contribution. Her plan of action—and the positive results—helped her feel like she had more control over her circumstances, and gave a big boost to her morale.

COACHING EXERCISE

If you're experiencing a frustrating lack of control in your work, what might you do about it?

Instead of descending into chronic complaining or fueling your resentful anger, examine the problem or conflict.

What would make it better?

What needs to be resolved?

Is there someone you can talk to about your concerns, who has influence within the organization?

Is there a possibility to adapt your schedule, or your tasks, to what would work best for you?

If you're not sure what to do, or are nervous about speaking to higher-ups, discuss your situation with a mentor or someone wise whom you respect.

---

3. Insufficient rewards

When we feel rewarded for our efforts at work, it gives us a boost that inoculates against burnout. Workplace rewards come in various forms: financial, institutional, and social. Leiter and Maslach state that "the associations between feelings of deprivation and burnout are prevalent."[14] If you're feeling deprived of your rightful rewards for your work, you're at risk. They also note that feelings of deprivation are more resistant to cognitive restructuring, which means that once you feel deprived (and presumably resentful or upset), it's hard to shake that, or shift that into a positive perspective.

Contribute to a culture of recognition and appreciation at your workplace. You can make a significant positive impact on your colleagues, and buttress them against burnout, by showing your appreciation. If you notice a quality that you admire in a coworker, or appreciate their efforts on a particular project, don't keep it to yourself. Let them know. Even better, tell them in a meeting, in front of others.

COACHING EXERCISE

If you're a leader, keep this issue of rewards top of mind.

What are you doing to ensure that your people

- *feel appropriately financially rewarded for their efforts?*

- *feel recognized by you and your organization for their positive contributions?*

- *experience rewarding interactions and connections with their colleagues and superiors?*

(Don't forget that as a leader you're at risk for burning out, as well. Managers can be at even higher risk for burnout than the people they lead. Take a look at the "if you're an employee" exercise below, and remember to apply those questions to yourself, too.)

If you're an employee and have been feeling deprived and unrewarded by your workplace, identify what's missing.

Are you way overdue for a raise?

Are you lacking positive feedback from your manager?

Do you feel disconnected from your coworkers?

Have you felt unappreciated by your clients or customers, or do you let even the slightest negative feedback get to you?

Are there steps you could take that might solve the issue(s)? (i.e., talking to your supervisor about a raise; asking your manager or coworkers to give you feedback regarding your strengths and things that you are doing well; making more of an effort to build closer, more rewarding relationships with the people around you; reminding yourself of positive feedback you have received from clients/customers and not letting the occasional complaint drag you down).

4. Lackluster community

The quality of your interactions with others at work has a direct impact on the relationship you have with the work itself. Leiter and Maslach sum this up powerfully: "A lively, attentive, responsive community is incompatible with burnout."[14]

When I speak to groups of leaders about preventing burnout in their people, I emphasize the importance of strong supervisory support. When people feel supported by their superiors, it makes them more resilient. This support can come in various forms: creating a culture of open, supportive, two-way communication; providing emotional support when people are struggling; or giving employees opportunities to grow and develop their skills.

Coworker support has been shown to make a difference, too. When people feel that their coworkers support and approve of them, their feelings of personal accomplishment and efficacy grow. This inoculates them against the third component of burnout.

Research from EY's Center for Talent Innovation demonstrates that when people feel like they belong at work, they're more productive, motivated, and engaged—and they're almost four times more likely to contribute to their fullest potential.[16] They also reported that people felt the greatest sense of belonging when their colleagues check in on them, both personally and professionally.

COACHING EXERCISE

Identify and ask for support.

First, identify what kind of support you need the most.

Do you need help from your supervisor in dealing with technical situations?

Do you need more emotional support and advice, in order to better handle stressful circumstances?

(If your manager isn't the type to give this support, see if you can find it somewhere else: a mentor, a colleague, another leader in the organization, a counselor, your spouse, a friend, etc.)

Are there trainings, certifications, or conferences that would help you grow and feel more inspired and capable?

Consider asking for what you need. Pick your battles and timing wisely.

COACHING EXERCISE

Be the change.

How can you help create that "lively, attentive, responsive community" culture?

If you're in a role of influence, how can you be a supportive, generous leader?

Encourage and support your coworkers. Be that person who energizes others. Bring those around you up, not down. Check in on the people around you. A simple "How are you doing?" or "How can I support you?" goes a long way.

Think of a colleague who you could check in on. Why not send them a message right now? (And if you'd rather check in with them in person, when might you do that?)

I witnessed an extraordinary, somewhat upside-down example of the latter, through one of my clients. Rebecca hired me because she was feeling tremendously burned out. She hated her job and wanted to get out as soon as possible. On her intake form, she wrote: "I hate my boss."

During the first month, we worked at improving her self-care outside of work (nutrition, sleep, exercise, fun). We built in firmer boundaries between her work and personal life. She started work a little earlier and then aimed to stop working by five o'clock every day, so that she could feel like she had more of an evening. She planned to go for a run when she finished work, which helped her to stop working on time and marked the moment when her workday ended and her personal life resumed. She also broke her habit of doing extra work in the evenings, shifting these tasks into her new earlier-morning work routine (she soon found that she got things done much faster in the morning compared to the evening, when she was tired). These steps immediately helped her feelings of resentment and being overwhelmed.

Next, we targeted her relationship with her boss, Fatima. Rebecca described Fatima as an intolerable individual. Critical, harsh, demanding, unfriendly, and a micromanager on top of that.

I worked at helping Rebecca cultivate compassion and a more open mind toward Fatima. She focused on improving the quality of her communications with Fatima, and started bravely asking for changes that she needed, in order to do her best work. Rebecca committed to speaking in a kind, friendly fashion, aiming to create connection, regardless of the tone that her supervisor brought to the conversation.

Things steadily improved. One day, Fatima walked into Rebecca's office and shut the door. She wanted Rebecca's advice.

Fatima explained, with uncharacteristic vulnerability, that she was facing a very difficult managerial situation and feared losing her job. Incredibly, Rebecca found herself providing emotional support and encouragement to someone who was starting to feel like a friend.

Eventually, almost a year had passed since Rebecca first hired me. Her symptoms of burnout were a distant memory, and she was still at the same job. One day, another organization attempted to headhunt her with a very appealing opportunity. Her response almost made me fall off my chair.

"I'm not sure I want to leave anymore," she told me. "It would feel disloyal. I would totally consider this other job—if only there was a way to bring Fatima with me."

The last I heard, she was still there, happily working alongside Fatima.

Extraordinary, right? If I'd told Rebecca that this would happen, when she first hired me, she wouldn't have believed me. Of course, it's not a guarantee that the same tactic would work with someone else in the future. Some people are too determined to be difficult.

Still, you never lose by treating people the way you want to be treated. You might be the person who sparks a change in your whole organization, you never know.

5. Unfairness

A fair leader is an effective leader. The same goes for an organization. Leiter and Maslach highlight the importance of this essential value: "Fairness is a quality of a strong community, especially in regard to distribution of rewards, opportunities and recognition."[14]

They recommend that leaders allocate resources and opportunities cleanly, based on organizational objectives, rather than favoring certain people or groups. As a leader, you might think that you can quietly get away with favoritism, but people will notice. And they will resent it.

If staff perceive their supervisors as being fair, they're more likely to accept organizational changes and are less vulnerable to burnout. Recall my client (the one who kept losing plum opportunities to less-qualified coworkers) who frequently thought about quitting her job in protest. Thankfully, she found a way to do something about the situation.

Be someone who advocates for fairness. Practice fairness in any areas where you have authority or control. If you witness unfairness, discrimination, or injustice, speak out about it or seek to remedy it (again, with wisdom and the counsel of wise mentors, whenever possible). If you're being treated unfairly, consider what you might be able to do about it.

6. Mismatch in values

Meaningfulness of work correlates with all three clinical dimensions of burnout. If your values align with how you spend your days, you'll be more energized, connected, and engaged, and you'll be more likely to feel proud of your accomplishments.

There's a catch, though. Leiter and Maslach point out that "idealistic expectations about organizations or their clientele predispose people to burnout, especially during initial phases of career development."[14]

I see this all the time in health care. We have pie-in-the-sky dreams that we'll be able to help everyone, and that we'll always feel rewarded and inspired by our work. Those dreams hit a wall, fast. You can end up profoundly disoriented and discouraged (and burned out from endlessly trying and hoping) if no one prepares you for it. Your passion and optimism will still give you a positive advantage, though, if you learn to keep them in a realistic perspective.

If you have the opportunity, find work that aligns with your values. You might also achieve this by requesting some changes to your job description or role, or a lateral move within your organization. If that's not possible, look for ways to find or create more meaning within your current role, or your life in general. (We'll talk more about creating meaning and purpose in the final chapter.)

PERSONAL RISKS FOR BURNOUT

First of all, it's a no-brainer that your choices or habits directly impact your risk for burnout. If you continually deprive yourself of sleep, eat poorly, never exercise, neglect your personal life, and rarely take breaks or time off, things won't go well. My goal is to help you implement solid habits, and lifelong practices and perspectives, that will make you more resilient.

You have less control over other personal risk factors. The primary components that make up your personality, according to the widely recognized "five-factor model" (extraversion/introversion, openness, neuroticism, agreeableness, and conscientiousness) are surprisingly stable across the lifespan.

Get ready—I'm about to describe the personality picture that's most at risk for burnout.[17] (Don't be overly upset if it sounds like you. I have most of these traits in spades, so you're in good company.)

1. High neuroticism

"Neurotic" is an awful word. I wish they'd chosen a different one for this personality trait, but there it is. People who score high in neuroticism tend to be anxious, insecure, and nervous. We find things to worry about, where others wouldn't even think to look. We're more likely to focus on the negative and minimize the positive. You can shift this tendency, though, and become less tense and edgy. If I can do this, anyone can! And I have. You can retrain the ingrained habit of focusing on the negative. This helps people with anxiety and depression, too (you'll find strategies and tips in Chapters 4 and 5).

Also, this isn't always a "born this way" thing. Our limbic systems, the fear and stress centers of our brains, can become overdeveloped or hardwired for negative reactions and tensions as a result of our experiences. Traumatic experiences can do this to our brains and our personalities. This happened to me, and it made me noticeably more neurotic and anxious. If this is your history, I recommend seeking trauma-informed counseling support to identify where and how this might be holding you back.

2. Introversion

Introverts aren't always easy to spot. You could be one, even though you don't wear glasses, aren't afraid to speak your mind, and no one ever describes you as "shy." I'm very introverted, but most people wouldn't guess it while talking to me or watching me speak onstage.

By definition, extraverts gain energy from interactions with others.

If they can't find a party, they'll host one. They love making up reasons to hold meetings. Try to like them anyway.

Introverts enjoy interactions with others (especially if the conversation is interesting or meaningful), but get drained by those interactions. If you're an introvert, you do best with a rhythm or schedule that lets you quietly recharge after a period of social contact.

I once worked with a client who wanted help with "overwhelming stress." I quickly identified her as an introvert after she told me that one of her biggest work-related stressors was the unrelenting social pressure. Her gregarious, extraverted coworkers constantly dropped by her desk to chat, invaded her coffee breaks, and insisted she join them at lunch. She had no time to recharge from her intensely social job as a manager, and she felt like she would perish from the pressure.

In retrospect, she might have been better off sticking to her initial career of accounting work, rather than accepting a socially demanding managerial role. In the meantime, I helped her take back and protect her downtime. She started slipping outside to enjoy her coffee breaks alone in a nearby park. She told her colleagues that she could only join them for lunch on Thursdays. Finally, she turned her train commute into an introvert-friendly, restorative oasis. Instead of answering emails, she put her work phone in airplane mode and listened to relaxing, restorative spa sounds through her earbuds.

3. Low (or extreme) conscientiousness

Conscientious types have a strong work ethic. If you're one of these, you're reliable and driven, and you take pride in doing good work. This can make you more resilient than your less-driven counterparts, and less prone to the burnout component of reduced accomplishment and efficacy. Most of my clients are extremely conscientious people; this makes them likely to be successful and also a delight to work with.

There's a dark side to being too conscientious, though. I see it all the time in my successful clients. Extreme conscientiousness can morph into crippling, whip-wielding perfectionism or impossibly high, stress-inducing standards. When I speak to groups of leaders, I often discuss the phenomenon of the "extra-miler."

In a *Harvard Business Review* article on "Collaborative Overload," the authors describe that extra-miler, an employee who routinely contributes above and beyond the scope of his or her role (read: an extremely conscientious person).[18] In excess, "what starts as a virtuous cycle soon turns vicious ... they are so overtaxed that they're no longer personally effective." Not only that, but extra-milers in an organization, who are seen as the best collaborators and top sources of information, will often have the lowest engagement and career satisfaction scores. As a result, these amazing, others-oriented, high-energy people become so depleted that they either burn out and become apathetic or end up leaving altogether.

By all means, work hard and contribute your best, but be wise about how and when. Be aware of this tendency in yourself, and hold it in reserve for when it's most needed. Only use it if you have the available energy. Hold back if you're feeling tired, and take care not to wear yourself out.

4. Low (or extreme) agreeableness

If you're warm, cheerful, and seek to get along with others, you probably score high on agreeableness. Less-agreeable people are more conflict-prone, less adaptable to change, less compliant, and more likely to have a pessimistic view of their job or their workplace (read: more vulnerable to burnout).

Again, though, I've seen the problems that come from being *too* agreeable. I work with burned-out, high-level executives, and you'd be amazed how many of these high-performing leaders struggle to say no to inappropriate requests for their time or attention. They're classic extra-milers, spread way too thin. They feel guilty about putting healthy, reasonable limits on how much they are willing to help or support others. Through my work with these leaders, I developed some of the work-focused boundary-setting strategies and tips that I share in

Chapter 8. In the next chapter, I share some essentials for cultivating the discipline of saying no.

As you can see, many different factors come together to set the stage for burnout. Use this knowledge to optimize your own circumstances. You can proactively prevent yourself from becoming another burnout statistic. You can also contribute to the increased awareness of burnout, and the driving factors, in your organization. Maybe you can even help shift the culture.

Make note of the risk factors that pertain to you, and take some time to do the related exercises in the downloadable workbook that accompanies this book. More than anything, commit to taking extraordinarily good care of yourself. We need you.

3

HOW TO STOP FEELING STRESSED AND OVERWHELMED

Linda, a successful health care professional in her early forties, hired me because she was "done." She had read my first book and knew that for a time I had ditched the city grind, moved to Mexico, and worked as a flamenco dancer and writer (in Chapter 4, I'll share that story with you). A single mother with a teenage daughter, Linda wanted to quit her job, move to South America, and spend her days writing and dancing tango. She thought I'd be the perfect person to help her leave her old life and build a shiny new one.

She was wrong. I turned out to be the perfect person to help her improve her current circumstances. When she finished her coaching program, she sent me an email to thank me, which included these comments about her experience: "I have found the space to focus on the things I really want to do. My desire to escape overseas to a new life dissolved. I found myself living the kind of life I no longer wanted to escape from."

Do you long to escape from your life? Do you feel like you're at your limit, but can't stop because you still have so much to get done? You look at your immediate future, and there's no end in sight, just an endless stream of demanding days. It feels like you'll never get to pause and breathe. I've been here—it's a terrible feeling. It's also very common, particularly among working parents.

I've worked with a long list of overwhelmed people. I've talked to many women and men who are overcommitted, stressed, and fried. They're under so much pressure, and they have so little free time. And even though they've asked me for help, they often share that they're worried that their situation is beyond repair.

Sometimes during an initial call with a client, I'll feel stressed just listening. I'll wonder, for a moment, if maybe they're right. Maybe I won't be able to help them. Thankfully, the vast majority of the time, things start turning around quickly, often by the second time we meet. It's amazing to watch. I'll share more of Linda's story, and how she transformed her life, at the end of this chapter, along with a simple framework that I've found really useful in helping crazy-busy people take back their lives and their health.

STRESS: A HEALTHY, BALANCED PERSPECTIVE

We need stress and work. We do best when we're stimulated and challenged in life. Stress makes us come alive and can bring out the best in us. Dr. Fricchione of Harvard's Benson-Henry Institute, in another course I attended in 2021, emphasized that intermittent, tolerable stressors (aka "hormetic" stressors) can enhance our physiological and psychological reserves.[1] He referenced Dr. Elissa Epel's paper on toxic stress and aging[2] that I mentioned in the introduction, noting that under-exposure to stress can lead to lack of development of "stress buffering resources." This, in turn, may hamper our ability to quickly recover from stressors.

Ideal exposure to sufficient numbers of manageable challenges throughout one's life can stimulate cognitive growth, coping skills, and emotion regulation skills. According to Epel, challenging experiences can "expand coping resources, knowledge, generativity, and feelings of accomplishment." Amazingly, the resulting phenomenon of "stress rejuvenescence" may even facilitate rejuvenation of your cells and tissues, leading to enhanced or "younger" biological functioning, along with increasing your overall resilience. It helps to remember that difficulties shape and strengthen us, when considering the different sources of stress in your life.

We shouldn't want to get rid of all the challenges in our lives. I don't dream about *la dolce vita far niente* (the sweet life of doing nothing) at retirement, because I know that doing "nothing" isn't good for humans. If my mind and body still work, I doubt I'll ever fully retire. Staying engaged in society, continually learning and using your mind and skills, will help keep you sharp, healthy, and happy as you age.

According to an analysis of the Health and Retirement Study, researchers reported that "complete retirement leads to 5–14 percent increase in difficulties with mobility and daily activities, 4–6 percent increase in illnesses and 6–9 percent decline in mental health."[3] These adverse effects can be mitigated by continuing to work part-time post-retirement. If you're someone who spends a lot of time hating on their job, and dreams of just checking out one day, you may want to rethink that vision. Work, and the structure it brings to our lives, is good for us mentally, physically, socially, and financially, as long as it's not excessively stressful.

When I look back on my career so far, my most cherished accomplishments all came with significant stress. A couple of times now, I've had the opportunity to share my thoughts and advice with millions of people via live national television on *The Today Show*. There's some preparation involved, but the interview isn't scripted and I could be asked almost anything. On the fly, I'll have a split second to formulate a coherent, useful response. It's high pressure and anxiety-provoking, and I feel really nervous the night before. At the same time, I feel so much passion and purpose in helping as many people as I can, and this is such a powerful way to reach people. When I'm finished and believe that I did my job well, it feels amazing. I faced a huge challenge and I did it! There's so much joy and accomplishment in that feeling.

Being pushed beyond our comfort zone, and rising to the occasion, strengthens us. Resilience only exists, and grows, through difficulties. If your life challenges you, that will likely bring out the best in you. You'll discover capacities and abilities you didn't even know were there.

Now if the stresses in our lives are continual, and regularly overwhelm our resources, that takes a toll. When the demands and stresses at work continually exceed your temporal, physical, mental, and emotional capacities to meet those demands, you can slide into burnout or depression.

We often can't control the demands on our lives. You may be a working parent with a demanding job, and aging parents to care for. That scenario can be extremely difficult and stressful. What you can do, though, is everything possible to increase your available personal and environmental resources that support you. These range from increasing your physical health and resilience, to making use of external community or government supports that are available.

I also will always encourage you, if you're struggling, to tap into qualified, professional support from your doctor, a counseling professional, a social worker, or whatever type of support would help you the most. Don't white-knuckle things on your own. Tapping into that full spectrum of resiliency resources will reduce your stress levels and optimize your ability to function well.

I also would caution here that if you have been diagnosed with a psychiatric condition such as moderate to severe depression or anxiety, bipolar disorder, psychosis, suicidality, or post-traumatic stress disorder (or have a history of trauma), do not try any of the stress-reduction techniques in this chapter without first discussing it with your doctor or counseling professional.

RECLAIM YOUR NERVOUS SYSTEM BY
CALMING YOUR STRESS RESPONSE

During busy times, I feel stressed and anxious when I wake up. I sit up in bed, turn on my phone, and plug in my headphones. Depending on what I feel like, I might pick a spiritually-oriented or mindfulness-focused app. I pick a recording to listen to and then breathe and actively relax, for at least ten minutes.

I've been doing a version of this practice since 2013, after the first time I attended the "Lifestyle Medicine: Tools for Promoting Healthy Change" course from Harvard's Institute of Lifestyle Medicine. That was the first time I heard Dr. Herbert Benson lecture on the Relaxation Response. I have my notes from that lecture open on my desk right now. Dr. Benson reported that up to 90 percent of health care visits are related to "mind-body stress-induced conditions."[4] Stress invokes the body's fight-or-flight response, which you've probably heard of. Stress hormones like adrenaline and cortisol pump through the body, blood pressure increases, your heart rate picks up, muscle tension rises, and you breathe more quickly and shallowly. This is useful when you've got to respond quickly to an acute threat, but isn't so great when your "threat" is a daily one, like a stressful job or difficult relationship.

The Relaxation Response, mediated by the parasympathetic nervous system, is the physiological opposite of the stress response. Mind-body techniques that induce the RR decrease stress-hormone release, lower blood pressure, slow the heart rate, help our muscles relax, and slow and deepen our breathing. According to Dr. Benson's research, if you induce the RR for just ten to twenty minutes, your nervous system becomes less reactive to stress. And the positive physiological stress-reducing effects can last for up to 24 hours. That's a rather incredible return on investment, no?

I should point out here that if you're in a genuinely challenging circumstance (and not just worrying about things that may or may not happen), the most effective way to reduce your stress is to address and improve or resolve the situation. I trust that some of the suggestions

I make throughout this book will be helpful to you in this, and again recommend that you reach out for professional support if you're struggling to make headway on your own. The stress-reducing techniques in this chapter function as an adjunct to your problem-solving process. They are tools to help you cope better—mentally, physiologically, and organizationally—with whatever is happening in your life.

TEACH YOUR BODY TO RELAX

The standard relaxation practice that Dr. Benson teaches involves choosing a word or sound in your original language. It could be "peace," or "rest," whatever—it really doesn't matter. Repetitive muscular activity works, too—the "runner's high" may be a result of the repetitive cadence of your feet triggering the Relaxation Response.

Sit quietly, and breathe in and out. With each breath, think of the phrase you are focusing on. When you notice that your mind wanders, calmly bring yourself back to your focus. The key here is to break your everyday train of thought, as this seems to be a significant driver of stress. I've heard Dr. Benson refer to this as "using the mind to shut off the mind." That may sound weird, but I assure you that unless you choose to introduce a spiritual element to this type of practice, this isn't a spiritual or religious phenomenon. It's pure mind-body physiology.

Do this for a minimum of eight minutes (ideally for ten to twenty), after which you can return to your normal thoughts. Go in and out of this practice slowly. Ideally you would do this daily, first thing in the morning, as I do. I've also had patients and clients do it in the evening before bed, as they find that it helps them sleep better.

This is one way to induce the Relaxation Response. There are lots of others, including a wide range of mindfulness and other relaxation techniques. There are several techniques that I use, and I'll talk about mindfulness in a moment. If I'm really stressed at any point in the day and can get away and be alone for a few minutes (you can even do this secretly, at your desk), I'll pop in my earbuds, put on an app that plays calming sounds, and just *breathe* for five to ten minutes.

It's immensely calming and so helpful.

And there's more: A regular relaxation practice comes with bigger benefits than just feeling calmer and reducing your body's reactivity to stress. As Benson and his colleagues have demonstrated, long-term practitioners of RR-inducing practices show enhanced expression of genes associated with the maintenance and protection of telomeres, suggesting slower aging and improved healing of cell damage, at a genetic level.[5]

That same study reported that not only is RR elicitation "an effective therapeutic intervention that counteracts the adverse clinical effects of stress in disorders including hypertension, anxiety, insomnia and aging," but that both short-term and long-term practitioners can evoke significant gene expression changes. They found that a twenty-minute audio-guided RR practice could enhance expression of genes associated with energy metabolism, mitochondrial function (mitochondria are our body's energy powerhouses), and insulin secretion, along with reduced expression of genes linked to harmful processes such as inflammatory and stress-related pathways. Put simply, your body loves when you induce its RR. It will reward you and your health for taking the time, in all kinds of amazing ways.

If you're pressed for time or in the middle of a stressful situation, try a "mini" or "micro" RR technique to calm your nervous system and reduce your body's stress response.

1. The 4-6-8 breath

There are lots of different ways to use your breath to stimulate your parasympathetic nervous system and induce calm. I like teaching this one, which goes like this:

- Breathe in through your nose for a count of four (not a full four seconds, just count it out).

- Hold your breath deep in your chest for a count of six.

- Breathe out through your mouth for a count of eight, releasing your stress through your breath as you exhale (if you're in public or in a stressful meeting, breathe out through your nose so no one can hear or notice what you're doing).

Do this once, or a few times in a row.

You can do this exercise at any time to calm your nervous system, whether you're actively dealing with stress or just bored—for example, when you're standing in line at the store, waiting for something to download, or stuck in traffic.

I used this type of breathing all the time with patients with high blood pressure. Their initial reading would be sky high. I'd have them take a couple of these breaths, and then show them the drop in their blood pressure. They'd be amazed, and they simultaneously learned a tool to manage stress and calm their cardiovascular system.

2.   The physiological sigh

This stress-reduction, RR-inducing technique that uses a "double inhale" has been studied and popularized by Dr. Andrew Huberman, PhD, a Stanford neurobiologist and neuroscience researcher:

- Take a breath in through your nose.

- Follow that immediately with a shorter second breath, inhaling through your nose once more.

- Exhale through your mouth.

Apparently the second breath pops open your alveoli (small air sacks at the periphery of your lungs). This allows more oxygen to penetrate your lungs, and also enables you to blow off more CO_2 with your exhale, resulting in significant reduction of the stress response.[6] I've tried this myself—it does feel very good, and I notice a calming effect.

REDUCE FEELING OVERWHELMED BY TRAINING
YOUR BRAIN TO FOCUS AND ADAPT

Mindfulness techniques are effective for stress reduction, and we've got reasonably strong data that supports the impact of mindfulness practices on our brains and neural functions.[7,8] I've also experienced it to be very helpful for me and for many of my patients and clients.

Meditation and contemplation have been practiced in different cultures and contexts for a very long time, and have associations with different religions and spiritual practices. I choose to conceptualize, practice, and teach on this topic neutrally, focusing on specific skills and the related psychological, physiological, and neurological benefits. I like these descriptions of mindfulness, from a paper on "The Neuroscience of Mindfulness Meditation": "non-judgemental attention to experiences in the present moment" and "practices that require both the regulation of attention (in order to maintain the focus on immediate experiences, such as thoughts, emotions, body posture and sensations) and the ability to approach one's experiences with openness and acceptance."[8]

In my experience, a formal mindfulness practice is a slightly different, expanded type of practice compared to the basic RR-inducing technique taught by Dr. Benson. Rather than just focusing on one thing like your breath or a word, the types of guided mindfulness practices that I enjoy (which could be categorized as a "focused attention" type of mindfulness practice) involve listening to an app-based audio recording that helps you focus and redirect your attention to various, shifting things. You may be guided to pay attention to the sensation of your breath, or areas of physical tension, or a general feeling of bodily rest. You might focus on sounds in the environment, or cultivating a sense of compassion for yourself or others, and so on. There are tons of mindfulness apps, audio recordings, and videos out there. Try different ones until you find something that works for you.

Again, if you're experiencing high levels of stress, these techniques aren't meant to replace important interventions like good old-fashioned problem-solving or receiving professional counseling, but there is evidence that they can help support you and may even help you discover solutions to your problems.

MIND-BODY MEDICINE AND NEUROPLASTICITY

Moderate to severe stress, over time, can increase the volume of the amygdala, the fear and stress center of the brain.[9] In one study, a group of stressed but otherwise healthy people participated in an eight-week mindfulness-based stress-reduction intervention.[10] After this training, not only did they report significantly reduced perceived stress, but this correlated with decreases in the density of the gray matter of the amygdala. Amazing.

I've been anxious since I was a kid. Maybe I was born that way, or maybe it was because of my environment—it's hard to say. I've also experienced a significant amount of work-related and personal stress, some of which resulted in trauma-related symptoms (for which I thankfully received effective treatment). My amygdala has been through the ringer. I get very excited about the potential for simple practices to help reverse that, so that my brain—and yours, too—becomes more physically resilient to stress.

Evidence also indicates that mindfulness practices improve your regulation of emotions. Negative emotions may become less intense, you may experience them less often, and you may become more likely to experience positive mood states.[8] This emotional stability helps a lot if your life is full of stressors and curveballs.

In response to the crises and stressors of the first year of the pandemic, I expanded my morning prayer and relaxation practice to include at least ten minutes of formal mindfulness meditation. Over time, I noticed a significant difference in my ability to stay calm during difficult conversations.

Because of negative past experiences, I used to feel a strong drive to shut down or leave whenever I felt unfairly attacked or criticized. Now I'm much more able to stay present. I can listen and then calmly defend myself or explain my position. I'm quite sure that the mindfulness practice is responsible for that, since I haven't really changed anything else. Also, the more positive experiences I have with my new skills, the less my brain fears or gets triggered by confrontation and difficult discussions. I'll talk more specifically about this phenomenon later, and will illustrate how you can cultivate similar shifts.

Finally, when you feel overwhelmed with problems and stressors, you need to be able to problem solve. This can be hard when your brain is exhausted or overwhelmed with stress hormones, as your executive function (cognitive processes that drive complex tasks, such as decision-making and goal-directed behavior) and memory can go offline. In addition to reducing that pesky stress hormone release, mindfulness practices have also been shown to improve creative problem-solving. For example, divergent thinking, a key aspect of creative performance which involves information retrieval, as well as coming up with a variety of responses to a certain problem, has been shown to improve with a short-term mindfulness-type intervention.[11]

Mindfulness practices can produce lots of other potential benefits that help you when you're overwhelmed and stressed, such as improving your focus and memory. I won't get into it all, but I think I've made my point that this can be an extremely helpful tool and adjunct to any other strategy you use to deal with a very stressful, too-busy life.

STAY PRESENT AND KNOW HOW TO REST

If you don't have time for, or interest in, a formal practice, try practicing mindful awareness as you move through your daily life. Recall that our everyday "train of thought" contributes to a lot of our stress. Whenever you're doing something specific, focus on that and don't let unrelated thoughts or worries hijack your mind or emotions.

If your mind wanders to work problems when you're hanging out with your kids, bring it back to focus on their sweet faces or voices. If you're in a meeting and someone's comment sends your brain down an unhelpful doomsday rabbit hole, bring your attention back to what's being discussed. If you train your brain to focus on what you're doing in the moment, and reserve worrying for times when you can actually think and plan constructively, you'll have so much less noise in your head, a better quality of life, and reduced levels of real and perceived stress.

Learn and practice how to rest in a variety of time frames and circumstances. Many busy people haven't taken the time to explore what works for them. It's common to think that you can only "really" rest when you're on vacation, take a day off, or are entirely alone. One of my clients, a leader who has young children, discovered that stealing some time to read a good novel in the morning (instead of reading the news or scrolling through social media), before the house wakes up, makes a difference to how her whole day feels. It might seem inconsequential to you, but it adds joy to her day and makes her feel more in control of her life. This type of intervention won't solve all your problems, but small doses of self-care do count psychologically, calm your nervous system, and add up. Do whatever works!

COACHING EXERCISE
Know what helps you relax, and do it.

For each of these time spans, list three things that you enjoy and that help you relax and unwind.

- **5 minutes** *(e.g., making a cup of tea; taking some deep breaths; doing some stretches; listening to a song that you like.)*

- **15 minutes** *(e.g., going for a quick walk; doing a mindfulness meditation; spending some time with a pet; texting with a friend to talk about your day.)*

- **30 minutes** *(e.g., calling a friend or family member to say hello; taking a bath; reading a book.)*

- **1 hour** *(e.g., taking an exercise class or dance class; going for a long walk; listening to your favorite album; painting, crafting, or some other creative endeavor.)*

I encourage you to keep a list of these in your phone or somewhere handy, and add to the list as things occur to you. Then, when you find yourself with a sudden spare few minutes or an hour, you can refer to what you've written so you don't end up wasting time scrolling through your phone (which is more likely to negatively impact your mood and energy) or watching some mindless show.

REDUCE CHAOS AND FIND MORE TIME BY KNOWING WHAT'S ESSENTIAL

Years ago, I read the book *Essentialism* by Greg McKeown,[12] a leadership expert who has studied and taught at Stanford Graduate School of Business. It changed the way I lived, and the way that I worked with clients.

You must know what's essential in order to know what to allow into your life and what to actively block. If you don't know this and fail to act on it, day by day your life will descend into chaos. If you're already there, fear not. This philosophy and strategy really works.

According to McKeown: "The way of the Essentialist means living by design, not by default. Instead of making choices reactively, the Essentialist deliberately distinguishes the vital few from the trivial many, eliminates the nonessentials, and then removes obstacles so the essential things have clear, smooth passage." If you're drowning in your life, this may sound impossibly lofty. Who has time to even stop and think about such things? You do. Really.

McKeown refers to the folly of "making choices reactively." When our lives are crazy busy, that's where many of us get stuck. We feel we don't have any control. We're just trying to keep our heads above water. So we power through, trying to hit every ball that comes flying in at us. We don't stop to think about what we're actually doing.

I've coached some of the busiest people in the world, clients who occupy high-level leadership positions in global organizations, work ninety-hour weeks, experience excruciating levels of performance pressure, and have small children at home. Yes, these are highly privileged, highly resourced people. They typically have good child-care and other types of domestic support. But their pace and their bigger life picture are still extreme and unsustainable. They contact me when they reach the point where they can't keep it all going anymore. They sense that it's all going to come crashing down unless they get some help.

Before we meet for the first time, I ask the client to make a short list of goals, describing the key changes they'd like to see in their life. That list tells me what matters to them. It typically includes improvements to mental and physical health, finding more time for themselves, exploring key career-related questions, and protecting time with people they love most (who they are usually spending little time with).

Next, we get to work prioritizing these essentials. We ruthlessly evaluate, eliminate, or block anything we reasonably can that's getting in the way of those all-important priorities. You'd be amazed by the number of "nonessentials" we discover and remove from their work lives, their personal lives, and even their thought patterns. I'll talk more about this process in a minute.

Once people put these practices into action, they start to find more time for what matters. Perhaps most importantly, they've taken time to think about and talk about what matters. It's now front of mind, and starts driving on-the-fly decisions about how to use their time. Quite quickly, they report feeling less stressed, more in control, and more nourished by their lives. And often, they make some big, long-overdue changes.

A STRATEGY TO HELP YOU TAKE BACK YOUR LIFE

Let's get back to Linda, my client who wanted to escape her life. She wasn't a world-class corporate overachiever, but she was stressed, overwhelmed, and unhappy with her day-to-day grind. How did she go from wanting to book a plane ticket to move to the other side of the world, to embracing and thriving in her current life?

We started small. A strategy that I use with many clients, inspired by *Essentialism*, involves identifying your top four essential life priorities

(McKeown focuses on having one overarching life priority, but I use this four-priority model for my coaching work). This isn't just a list of goals. You step back and reflect on what really matters to you, beyond the superficial and the daily demands of life. In doing so, you verbally and psychologically commit to protecting those things as absolute top priorities. This process announces: "I'm going to start *choosing* what matters, even if that looks impossible to me right now."

According to McKeown, "When we forget our ability to choose, we learn to be helpless. Drip by drip we allow our power to be taken away until we end up becoming a function of other people's choices—or even a function of our own past choices. In turn, we surrender our power to choose." You'd be surprised by how many aspects of your life that seemed fixed or "necessary" are just past or ongoing choices that aren't actually necessary. They take up space and cause needless stress.

At this point, you might feel worried that this is about becoming more selfish. Maybe you worry about putting yourself first and others last, avoiding commitments, and refusing to help other people. It's a fair concern. It's good to examine our hearts, motives, and character. I've found, though, that people who worry about being selfish usually aren't capable of being pathologically so. Narcissists, for example, don't worry about the impact of their choices on others. If you're like most people I work with, you're excessively generous with your time. You're excessively focused on what others think and need, to the point that you've compromised your health and stretched yourself near your breaking point. Refocusing your priorities, especially for the sake of your mental health, your physical health, and the things that matter most, isn't selfish. Your increased well-being will likely benefit those closest to you. And you'll be better positioned to make a meaningful contribution to your world.

Linda felt chronically exhausted. She powered through her days by using sheer will, navigating an endless list of demands and to-do's, with no time to stop and think, reflect, or rest. As her top priority, she wanted to improve her general health and energy. Next, she specifically wanted to focus on eating better and to cook more as part of that. Third, she longed to have time to cultivate relationships with the people who mattered most to her. She also dreamed of finding something she could be really passionate about. These things really mattered to her.

Once you're identified your essential priorities, it's time to actually live like they're your priorities. First, identify what's getting in the way.

When we first examined Linda's life, she lived in a large city. She hated the lengthy commute to the health care center where she worked long hours. The little free time she had was filled with social commitments, which she felt pressured to participate in. She felt she had no time to take care of herself or to connect with her daughter.

We started with simple improvements to her health-related habits (you'll find lots of tips to help you do the same, in the chapters on sleep, food, and exercise). She stopped using late-night binge-watching as a way of coping with stress, and she went to bed earlier. She wanted to eat more vegetables, but struggled to find time to shop. When I asked her what she might do, she decided that she could sign up for a local vegetable-box delivery service. She hated to waste anything, so being forced to eat a box of veggies would be just the thing to get her eating better.

A variety of vegetables started arriving, including some she'd never tried before. She researched recipes to prepare these novel foods, and discovered that she loved making and eating new dishes. She'd always been so busy (and grabbing takeout or frozen meals) that she didn't even know she liked to cook. She discovered so many delicious new recipes, that she started inviting friends over to help her eat the vegetables.

Linda valued exercise, but never had time for it. Beyond all her work hours, a wide network of people packed her calendar with invitations and obligations. "Essentialists," by definition, get really good at saying no. So, we focused on this. First, she had to practice identifying and saying no to things that she didn't want to do or need to do (you'd be surprised by how many of these creep into people's lives).

The breakthrough secret, though, lay in the next step. Inspired by McKeown's philosophy, I encouraged Linda to start saying no to things that sounded fun or even amazing. If they weren't on her top priority list, they weren't allowed to steal time from her essentials. Later, Linda told me that *really* learning when and how to say no made the largest impact on her life. Quite quickly, she was able to free up time to sign up for the tango classes she'd longed to take. She felt fit, healthy, and more alive than she had in years, and she had more time for her daughter. She also had time to think more deeply and strategically about her life.

Her metropolitan life was expensive. She often took extra work shifts to help pay the bills. Her daughter decided to attend university in a neighboring state, in a sweet college town with an excellent teaching hospital and a lower cost of living. Linda took the leap. She applied for and got a job at that teaching hospital, sold her cramped city condo, rented a cute little townhouse, and found some local dance classes. She was still close enough that on her days off, she could visit her best city friends.

Now that she didn't have to commute anymore, she also had time to write a book. This turned out to be the passion she'd been searching for. I still remember the wonder I felt, when she told me about the book. What a transformation. Over the course of a year, I had watched this all from afar, jumping up and down and cheering her every move.

I know, you may not relate to her story. As a single professional with an established career and an older child, Linda may have much more flexibility or access to opportunities and resources than you do. Don't let this discourage you. In my medical psychotherapy work with patients, I have counseled and coached patients from all sorts of circumstances. You'd be surprised at what changes are possible for you, even if you just start by taking better care of yourself in small ways, and opening your eyes to the potential resources and opportunities around you. Be alert for ways that you might be able to change your circumstances or your environment.

COACHING EXERCISE

Apply the top four priority framework to your life.

1. Identify what's most important to you right now.

Your health? Your mental health? Your family? Feeling less stressed and more engaged at work? Switching careers? Be specific. Write these things down in a list.

Once you have a list, decide which items are in your "top four" by putting a star by each one, and then write them out in order.

(If this is difficult to come up with, try thinking of what you resent most right now. What are you most frustrated about? Your weight? Your health? How tired you are? Being unable to spend quality time with your spouse or kids? Feeling stressed about debt?)

2. Determine what you want and need to start doing to honor these priorities.

Identify which of your top priorities are suffering the most right now (circle one or more).

For each area that is suffering, come up with one way to give that more time and attention. Write it down next to that priority.

Be specific. Some examples: going to bed at ten o'clock; going for walks with a friend three times a week after work; planning a date night once a week with your partner; spending Saturday mornings with your kids; signing up for that photography course you've always wanted to take.

Pro tip: Keep it simple at first—aim for easy wins.

3. Identify the greatest obstacles in your life that are preventing you from taking care of or finding time for your priorities.

Take a look at your calendar for the next month. What can you realistically remove?

Is there anything on there that's not truly necessary, or that you dread or feel stressed about, such as social obligations (e.g., the ones that you regularly find tiresome, stressful, or draining)? Unnecessary commitments (e.g., that committee you joined ages ago, where you don't really do anything meaningful and you kick yourself every time you lose another Thursday night to a meeting)?

Have you been wasting time on activities that have nothing to do with your priorities or that sabotage those priorities? What could you remove that's less important than your identified priorities?

If there's something in your life that you long to be rid of, get creative about ways that you might finally be able to be free of it.

Talk to someone you respect about the situation, if you feel stressed or guilty about making this change. They may help you give yourself permission to stop participating in this activity, relationship, or commitment.

4. Brainstorm how you can start to remove these obstacles.

Identify the low-hanging fruit; what are the easiest things for you to remove from your life? What can you easily start saying no to? What can you delegate to someone else or remove from your plate?

What in your life, or your work, might you be able to change?

What are some of the resources around you that you could leverage to help take a load off, or help you achieve your priorities? Who might you ask for help?

(For example, if you're caring for aging parents, or have a child who faces significant challenges, have you fully explored the resources that may be available in your community to support you or your loved ones?)

5. Cultivate your ability to say no.

Take your list from #4. Look over the things you could easily say no to, and start there.

As you think about saying no, notice what comes up for you.

What feelings or thoughts make you tempted to just cave in and say yes? Guilt? Fear of conflict? Fear of someone getting angry or upset with you? Fear of what people will think or say about you? It's important to understand what has been stopping you from doing what you know you need to do.

Practice different ways of saying no. If it's too hard for you in person (maybe you panic and abandon your resolve, or you're afraid to see the person's reaction), start by turning down requests in writing through text or email. These means of communication can make you feel more in control, as you can really think about and craft your responses.

*When you're tempted to just give in and say yes, remind yourself of **why** it's so important for you to stand your ground. What will you lose, how will your life suffer, and who else will suffer if you say yes to this?*

Take accountability if you're really struggling with implementing this. Perhaps you could make a pact with a friend that you're both going to start saying no to certain things, and check in on each other for strength, resolve, and encouragement. A counselor can help you with all of this as well (from exploring your reasons for feeling you have to say yes, to implementing new strategies and skills in saying no).

When it comes to identifying and protecting your priorities, brainstorm as many possibilities and solutions as you can. Invite trusted others to chime in with their suggestions, too. You'll be surprised by how much in your life can be improved when you know and commit to your priorities, start saying no, consistently make choices that honor what matters most, and tap into the resources that are all around you.

PART III

FORTIFY YOUR MENTAL HEALTH AND WELLNESS

4

UNDERSTAND DEPRESSION AND ENJOY MORE GOOD DAYS

The night felt like it would never end. Fighting to keep my eyes open, I admitted one critically ill patient after another into the hospital's Cardiac Care unit. I went through the motions of examining patients, writing orders, and calling attending physicians. As I did, I fervently hoped that the bulky "Code Blue" pager, which hung heavily from the waistband of my hospital greens, would never go off.[1]

Whenever I could grab a few rare minutes, I retreated to the windowless cell of my "call room" and lay on the rough, antiseptic sheets of the small, hard bed. Cold and uncomfortable, I longed to sleep but

---

[1]   This story, which has been adapted for this book, first appeared in *Live a Life You Love: 7 Steps to a Healthier, Happier, More Passionate You.*

couldn't, as a stream of footsteps and squeaking stretchers rushed down the hallway outside my door.

When I finally walked out the sliding hospital doors at the end of my shift, it was already dark again. Throughout the endless 36-hour shift, I'd dreamed of going home, yet when I finally opened my front door and dropped my bags on the floor, I came home to nothing. I lay down on the carpet, right next to where I'd thrown my bags, and sobbed.

I had no idea how I was going to get through the rest of the week, much less the full five years of the ER residency I was in. I felt like I had nothing to look forward to, nothing to live for. No reason to go to bed and wake up the next morning. When I opened my eyes, I'd just go back for more of the same.

I'd been diagnosed with depression by my doctor, but I now can see that I was simultaneously suffering from severe burnout. I also felt weirdly anxious. I'd seen such tragic and traumatic things during my shifts in the ER. Years later, I discovered that the new edginess that I felt during residency was probably related to post-traumatic stress.

One night, after I'd witnessed the death of a child, I didn't even try to sleep. I paced up and down the hospital halls, trying to rid myself of the images and the feelings. The neurosurgeon who'd been involved in that situation walked past me at one point. "Some nights are rougher than others, aren't they?" he said, and kept on walking. At least he'd said something to acknowledge what had happened, but it didn't help much.

The only treatment I'd been given for all of this was antidepressant medication. Not surprisingly, given the complexity of what was actually going on, the pills only helped a little. They didn't address the root issues. It stuns me today, knowing what I do about mental health, that no one ever recommended counseling. I'd also never been offered any debriefings at work, with respect to some of the traumatic situations. Nobody really talked about the extreme, difficult, and sometimes even personally risky circumstances that we dealt with in the ER. If they did, it was usually in an excited tone, because a situation had been novel or clinically challenging. We just kept soldiering on.

As I lay on the floor of my apartment that night, I couldn't fully grasp the various factors that were contributing to how I felt. I didn't really understand why everything felt so awful. Maybe you've felt like that, too. Maybe even recently. Maybe you don't know how you're going to be able to continue. Maybe you can't see how things are ever going to change for you. It can feel like there aren't any options and that there isn't any hope.

I assure you, there is. And please, be wiser than I was back then. I hid what was going on, from everyone other than my doctor. I would still recommend talking to your doctor, but reach out for additional support. Get counseling, talk to people who love you, tap into whatever resources you have available to you.

Life is full of surprises and good things that you couldn't have anticipated. Hang on, take care of yourself, and take one small step toward healing at a time. I know it can be hard to believe that things will get better, when things feel so tough and you're exhausted. It can be close to impossible for an exhausted, anxious, depressed brain to accurately assess the truth of your reality and the hope of your future.

Thinking about my options that night, I didn't know how to do anything other than be a doctor. I couldn't think of any other way that I could survive in this world (it's obvious to me now that I had all kinds of options, but I couldn't see any of them in that dark moment).

There was only one way out that I could see. At that very moment, as I lay there considering "exit" options (such as the medication in my bathroom cabinet), the phone rang. It was one of the Senior Emergency Medicine residents, a woman named Karen who'd always been very kind to me. She'd never called me before. And in the state I was in, it was quite something that I even answered the phone.

"How are you doing, Susan?" she asked me. "I've noticed that you haven't seemed yourself lately. Is everything all right?"

An expert at projecting perfection, I instantly slapped my mask on.

"I'm fine, thanks," I responded, cheerfully. "How are you?" She didn't let me get away with it, and kept asking me questions in her warm, curious way. I gradually relaxed, and then she dropped a bombshell.

"The main reason I'm calling is because I want to talk to you about something. Did you ever hear about the resident who took her life a few years ago?"

I had. The ER was an intense, competitive environment where I'd learned, even while preparing to apply for the residency, that you don't show weakness. Sadly, the things that I'd heard said about this individual weren't kind. Jokes were made. I suppose that was some people's way of coping with what had happened, but still.

She went on. "Well, I thought it might be important for you to know that she took her life at the exact point in her residency where you are now, in second year, during her Cardiac Care unit rotation." She paused to let that sink in, and then continued. "I'm going to ask you one more time. How are you, really?"

Finally, that mask that I'd worn for so long fell off and shattered into a thousand pieces around me. I told Karen everything: that I believed I'd made a mistake choosing emergency medicine as a specialty; that I'd had enough of the huge workload, the enormous stress, and the lack of sleep; that antidepressants had helped at first, but didn't seem to be working anymore.

She then said something that no one had ever said to me.

"You know, Susan, you don't have to do this if you don't want to."

Never once had I considered that. The long forgotten and ignored "me," the one who was crying her eyes out, couldn't imagine saying how she really felt about everything—or that she might have a say in anything. Since I was a kid, I'd let the overachieving, people-pleasing "super-me" drive the bus. I'd ignored my true preferences and needs for so long that I didn't even know what they were.

Karen pointed out that I had just about enough credits to get my general license as a physician. I didn't have to continue in the ER if I didn't want to. I'd had no idea! She also told me to go to my doctor and get an immediate stress leave.

Her final sentences still ring in my head today. She gave me two things to reflect on during my time off. First, she asked me to think about what my true interests really were. "And also," she continued, "I want you to think about what you'd like your life to be like—what you really want to do with your life."

The next day, I went to see my doctor. She wrote me a note for seven weeks of stress leave, a gift so mind-boggling to an overworked, sleep-deprived resident that I could hardly believe it was happening. I still didn't know what I might actually want to do with my life. I wasn't sure that I'd ever find the courage to leave my residency. After a few days of rest, though, I did know one thing: I wanted to go to Cuba. I had come across a local travel deal for a week at a modest all-inclusive resort, and I booked it (with the help of funds from my student line of credit).

In Cuba, I sat by the pool, fascinated by the other tourists. Watching them and chatting with some of them, I felt as if I'd suddenly woken up. I'd spent eleven years in university by then. The last six years, I'd spent almost all my time with medical students, residents, and doctors, and absorbed the idea that it was normal to work around the clock, sleep in scrubs, and focus my life on textbooks, facts, and diseases. In Cuba, I was surrounded by people celebrating with their friends and families. They shared stories of other vacation adventures and the fun things they did at home. These people had lives outside of work. And some of them even liked what they did! The contrast between their lives and mine shook me deeply.

I'd brought along a journal, in case I didn't make any friends and spent all my time alone (I wanted to have something "to do" while sitting by the pool or in the restaurant). I didn't end up having much time to write, but while writing one entry I watched myself pen a surprising sentence: "I want to be a writer."

I had almost no experience with writing, and had taken only the minimum required arts courses in university. Essays would mean that professors could grade me based on their whims or moods, something much too risky for my perfect GPA. And now I want to be a writer? It seemed bizarre and totally out of character. Yet I was willing to consider anything at that point. Desperation isn't fun, but it can be a great motivator.

Then, one night, I chose a seat at the back of a little open-air theater and waited for the evening's show to start. If I close my eyes, I can put myself right back in that chair, and can relive every detail of what happened next.

The lights dimmed, and a spectacularly alive mix of horns, percussion, and piano music blared from the speakers. Then came the moment I'll never forget: a sensational team of Cuban salsa dancers exploded onto the stage. As I watched them, a long-buried memory burst forth into my mind.

A little girl who was obsessed with dancing.

If you had asked me when I was around eight years old what I wanted to be when I grew up, I would have told you immediately.

"In the daytime, I'm going to be a journalist. Or maybe write books. But at night, I'm going to be a *Solid Gold Dancer*."

If you're too young to know what I'm talking about, I would advise against Googling the latter. I don't think my parents knew that I was watching this rather adult-oriented dance show on TV. They for sure didn't know that I was imitating the dance moves in the basement—to the tune of my stack of ABBA records—almost every night. Since my parents wouldn't put me in dance lessons (they had their reasons), I had to take matters into my own hands. I needed to be ready. I was sure that when I grew up, I would be a dancer, too.

By the time I was ten or so, my teachers were excited to discover that I was "gifted" in the sciences. From that point onward, life revolved around school: studying, getting straight A's, and getting as much praise from the adults around me as possible. I finally had their attention. I decided that academic achievement, not dancing, must be my destiny.

And it was. I support encouraging bright young girls and women to consider all possibilities for their future careers. I'm really grateful for all the encouragement, support, and fantastic opportunities that I got. What went wrong, however, was that I turned my academic accomplishments, and my choice of career, into my identity. The decision to apply to medical school was directed and decided by a conversation with a well-intentioned professor. It wasn't my idea, but it was what someone with my grades should do, so I did it.

By the time I was lying on that floor during my ER residency, there was nothing left of me, or my life, but work. I'd forgotten and ignored that little dancer, along with all the other important aspects of life that make us fully human—the essential aspects of a whole life that would have helped to preserve my mental health. It wasn't all on me, though, as the inhumane sleep deprivation, pressure, and pace of residency training has a famously brutal effect on mental and physical health. It leaves little room for those important other aspects of life. Our context matters.

Maybe you have left the more human parts of you behind, in your pursuit of success in the corporate world, or your chosen field. Maybe that's why you picked up this book. You know that the way you're prioritizing and living your life needs to change. If you're like I was, if you've stopped taking care of yourself and doing the things that give your mind and body life, let's change that. I wrote this for you, for this time in your life right now.

After my epiphany in Cuba, I went home and resigned from my residency. I completed the credits required to obtain my general license to practice medicine in the community, and worked in urban clinics for twenty years. As I mentioned earlier, I also spent time working in medical psychotherapy, supporting patients who were experiencing anxiety, depression, and extreme stress during the first year of the COVID-19 pandemic. I still have a medical license, but right now, as I write this, I'm working full time in what I believe to be my primary calling: mental health and resilience education, focused primarily on speaking to organizations, and using writing to increase awareness. I still do some executive coaching as well; I really enjoy this work, and it gives me an insider's perspective on what's happening in the real world of work, across various sectors. This informs my educational efforts, highlighting how I might be able to impact organizational cultures and systems on a larger scale.

I should mention something here. Many clients come to me feeling burned out and disillusioned with their work, and wanting a change. They often think that means quitting. They know my story and want help navigating their transition. Thankfully, new jobs take a while to find.

We typically have a good chunk of time to work on their current circumstances. We actively improve their boundaries and other ways in which they relate to their work. I get them sleeping and exercising again, and help them prioritize key relationships and activities. Soon, their lives feel more balanced and humane. As I mentioned in the chapter on burnout, most people I work with recover their affection for their work when they take these various steps, and don't end up quitting their jobs. In my case, though, I truly wasn't suited to a career in emergency medicine. It wasn't the right place for me, and it never would be.

After I returned from Cuba, I also signed up for salsa dance lessons. I eventually joined a couple of performance salsa dance teams, taught workshops, and even performed on television. That little girl who loved sparkly costumes would have been beside herself with excitement at her grown-up self's dance accomplishments. I eventually fell in love with and transitioned to Spanish flamenco dancing, took several courses in Spain, and had my own little flamenco and salsa dance company in Los Cabos, Mexico, where I lived for a few years. That is a story for another day!

While all this was unfolding, I committed to learning everything that I could about "whole person" health, wellness, mental health, and resilience. The more I learned, the more I felt called to share that knowledge and hope with the world, through speaking, writing, and working with the media. And here I am right now, writing this and doing what I love most in the world. As part of that mission, I'd like to share with you some of the key things I've learned about mental health, and mental wellness, along the way.

Before I do, I want to reemphasize that the content of this chapter (and this book) is intended to increase knowledge and awareness. It should never replace the process of diagnosis, advice, and treatment from your doctor. It is not intended to be applied to severe or complex mental health conditions. If you're struggling with your mental health, please reach out to a fully qualified, licensed professional, such as your doctor or a psychologist, for assistance and support.

THE DIFFERENCE BETWEEN DEPRESSION AND A "NORMAL" LOW MOOD

Life is tough. It will always have ups and downs. You'll have good days, bad days, and good and bad weeks. Though it's normal to want to be happy all the time, it isn't normal to feel happy all the time. Understanding that can take a lot of pressure off your life. A bad day or week isn't something to be feared. It's okay to feel down sometimes, to allow those feelings to be, versus fighting them or pushing them down. Negative emotions can point us to things we need to change, such as taking better care of ourselves, reducing time with someone who isn't good for us, or booking a much-needed vacation.

There is a point, though, where doctors become concerned about a low mood. According to the American Psychiatric Association, "depression (major depressive disorder) is a common and serious medical illness that negatively affects how you feel, the way you think and how you act."[1] Typically, you would experience the symptoms of depression every day or nearly every day, for a period of at least two weeks. This should also be experienced as a noticeable change from your previous level of functioning.

Symptoms of depression can include:

- Feeling sad, down, or depressed

- Loss of interest and enjoyment in things that you normally enjoy doing

- Appetite changes (increased or decreased appetite, with related unintentional weight gain or loss)

- Changes in sleep, either difficulty sleeping or spending more time sleeping than usual

- Decreased energy levels or increased fatigue

- "Psychomotor" speeding or slowing—finding it hard to sit still, or moving or talking much more slowly

- Difficulty concentrating

- Thoughts of ending one's life

I want to emphasize that if you're experiencing depression, it's not something to feel ashamed of. First of all, it's extremely common. According to the same reference from the American Psychiatric Association, one in six people will have an episode of depression at some time in their life. Depression also affects women more than men. Some studies show that up to one-third of women will experience a major depressive episode at some point in their life.[1]

We need to be aware of the symptoms, and take action if we're concerned that we (or a loved one) are depressed. This starts with seeing a doctor, especially if someone is feeling suicidal. Serious suicidal thoughts are considered a medical emergency that needs immediate action and attention; call a crisis line or go to an ER if you can't get in to see a doctor.

If you're experiencing depression or low moods, please have lots of compassion for yourself. This, too, shall pass—and there are lots of simple things that can be done to make it better.

WHAT CAUSES DEPRESSION?

Not all cases of depression are created equal. There can be many different root causes. Depression can "run in families"; in these cases, there may be a shared genetic vulnerability or intergenerational trauma. Some medications or medical conditions can bring on symptoms of depression, as can major life stressors or changes such as job loss, financial stress, chronic work-related stress, or relationship losses.

Once medical and other treatable causes have been identified or ruled out, there are some common depression-provoking factors. These can keep you stuck, or cause depression to get worse. A qualified psychologist or counselor can be very helpful here to encourage you in the thoughts and choices that will help you get back to feeling like yourself again. Cognitive behavioral therapy (CBT), a counseling technique that helps you change both thoughts and behaviors, is powerfully effective in treating depression.

A team of clinical psychologists in my region created an excellent, freely available resource that's designed to help people develop *Antidepressant Skills at Work*.[2] I particularly appreciate their explanation of the causes of low mood and depression. They depict depression as a cycle, with five main causes that drive it. Each of these five elements can cause depression and can keep the depression cycle going (each can also be leveraged to stop the cycle and move you toward healing).

Here is that list of causes, along with some of my thoughts, experiences, and recommendations related to each area.

1. Situations

If a situation like job loss, isolation, relationship conflict, or ongoing specific stress is what caused your depression, you must address this. Get support from a counselor, coach, support group, or wise friend or family member to help you improve your coping skills and strategize around improving or changing the situation.

2. Thoughts

I often say that a depressed mind makes up lots of lies. "I'm worthless," "Nothing's going to change," or "No one would miss me if I wasn't around" are common inaccurate, depression-related thoughts. Challenging situations or negative emotions will fuel these negative thoughts. If you're tired or chronically stressed, it's hard to think clearly. It's easy to slip into distorted negative thought patterns. Again, get help to shift the distorted thoughts that perpetuate a low mood. CBT can help a lot in getting you out of a negative thought rut. There are CBT workbooks out there, too, that contain exercises to help you work on this.

3. Emotions

When you're depressed, you experience a variety of negative emotions. These also result from a variety of triggers, including stressful situations, negative thought patterns, sleep deprivation, inactivity, or isolation. You may feel chronically discouraged, sad, anxious, or irritable. Some people feel numb or flat. Thankfully, small things can help move you out of these feelings. Talking to a counselor can bring relief or renewed hope. Intentional actions, such as journaling, praying, taking time to physically care for yourself, or spending time with people you love, can make a real difference (more about helpful actions in a moment).

4. Physical state

The mind-body connection plays a significant role in causing and perpetuating depression. Antidepressants work at this level, shifting the biochemistry of the brain. While I don't advocate using medication as a single, isolated approach to depression (it's important to treat depression from the whole person perspective I'm describing here), I've seen antidepressant medication change lives. A friend of mine who had struggled with depression for years finally decided to try medication. She told me that it was like someone "flipped a switch" inside her. She has felt enormously better ever since. Her family has a strong history of depression, so there could be a significant genetic component to her condition.

Other physical changes that can accompany depression, such as an inability to sleep, make you feel worse if left unaddressed. A low appetite typically leads to skipping meals. This can cause low blood sugar that makes you feel weepy or "hangry." Cravings for junk food can cause you to eat foods that irritate your brain. You also miss out on important nutrients that would help your brain feel better. It's important to understand these dynamics and take actions (and receive treatment) that reduce these physical drivers of depression and start to reverse their impact.

5. Actions

Here you can really take back your power, and reverse the cycle of depression. When you're depressed, it's common to withdraw socially and decrease your activity level. You stop taking care of yourself in a variety of ways. This drives the downward spiral of depression.

Small positive actions can really change the way you feel. Make basic self-care your starting point. It goes a long way. Here are some things you could do to shift the balance of your mental health: force yourself to take a shower; put on proper clothes (even if no one will see you); eat simple healthy meals (even if you're not hungry); go out for a walk; make sure you have groceries in your house; reconnect with your faith community and receive their support; accept that invitation for coffee with a good friend (even if it's the last thing you feel like doing). Notice how much better you feel after you take one of these actions. You'll feel better about yourself, too.

Of course, all of these things would be too much to do at once. Start with whatever is easiest. Don't wait until you feel like doing it—just do it. Every single time you go against the negative pull of depression and do something to take care of yourself, you nudge the wheel in the direction of health and recovery.

It's ideal to work together with a counselor to identify small changes, set goals, and take accountability. I've also seen people with mild depression make these changes on their own because they know that they "should" and that these small actions will help.

COACHING EXERCISE

Identify key actions to optimize your self-care.

Regardless of whether or not you're depressed, it's always a good idea to take good care of yourself, in ways that matter to you.

Write a list of actions that make you feel better about yourself or give you a lift (e.g., taking a shower in the morning, going for a daily walk,

> *having a supply of healthy food, dressing nicely even if you're not leaving your home on a given day, etc.)*
>
> *Pick one that you'd like to work on doing every day this week, if that's possible.*
>
> *Now do these actions over the course of the week, and notice how much better you feel.*

DRUG-FREE WAYS TO BOOST YOUR MOOD

After my experience of depression and burnout in residency, I made so many changes to my life and the way that I lived. I made sure I actually *had* a life. I believe that really helped me to be able to stop the antidepressants within a year or so. So far, I haven't had to take them again. It's been over twenty years since that night in the ER, so that's a pretty good track record!

I committed, after that terrible season, to learn everything I could about the daily choices that lead to better mental health. I promised myself I would consistently make mental health–promoting choices in all aspects of my life, for the rest of my life. These actions don't replace first-line treatments for more severe depression, such as CBT and antidepressants, but they've helped me a lot. Here are some of the evidence-based actions that I regularly engage in to stay well:

1. Live a physically active life (move every day if you can).
Dancing healed my life. You'll recall that when I returned from that trip to Cuba, I signed up for salsa lessons. That turned into years of dancing. I went from having almost no exercise during my residency, to taking salsa classes two nights a week and going out dancing two to three nights a week. Later, when I pivoted to flamenco, I followed a similar pattern of frequency and intensity.

Those dance-obsessed years were the most joyous of my life. If you're a working parent with young kids, I get that you don't have time to immerse yourself in hours of dancing. But regular exercise will have a powerful impact on your mood and energy levels.

Increased physical activity is connected to lower rates of depression.[3] One study showed that women suffering from major depression experienced significant relief of symptoms with a once-weekly 30-minute exercise session.[4] The authors commented that "exercise of any intensity significantly improved feelings of depression," and that "acute exercise should be used as a symptom management tool to improve mood in depression."

Try to do something physical every day. It could be a walk outside, or taking the stairs at your workplace whenever you can. Not only will you boost your mood, but you'll enjoy the other benefits of exercise that I'll discuss in more detail in Chapter 11, including improved emotional resilience, better ability to maintain a positive mood under stress, improvement of burnout symptoms, and increased overall resilience of your brain.

2. Do things that bring you joy.

When life's a grind, everything feels like a chore. If your brain's constantly under stress, it gets entrenched in negative pathways. Positive neurotransmitters get depleted and your baseline mood becomes low.

Break this cycle and enhance the state and mood of your brain by intentionally tuning into joy. Here are some suggestions:

- When you're out for a walk, take time to appreciate any beauty around you. Stop to admire and smell flowers. Enjoy the feel of the sun on your face.

- Spend time in nature whenever you can. Take time to notice how beautiful it is, or how peaceful. Whatever makes you feel good.

- Play with children. Don't just go through the motions, get into it. Be silly. Laugh with them. Laugh at them.

- Seek out feel-good, inspiring, or humorous movies and books. Stop to watch and laugh at the silly videos that your friends post or send to you.

COACHING EXERCISE

Practice joy.

- *List five things that bring you joy (simple things that ideally are easily accessible in your daily life).*

- *In your calendar, plan out one of these per day over the next five days, so that you will be reminded to do it.*

- *Notice how much better these "touchstones of joy" make you and your life feel.*

3. Spend time with people.

Healthy relationships are the greatest determinant of health and happiness. When we're depressed, sad, burned out, or feeling low, it's natural to withdraw socially and start avoiding people. Guard against this! In your most difficult times, you need people the most.

Boost your mood and strengthen your mental wellness by intentionally spending time with people you enjoy. Make it a priority. Oh, the number of times I've felt too tired to hang out, or regretted a pre-booked social commitment after a busy day (recall that I'm an introvert). If I'm not completely wiped out, I'll usually make myself go. I know it will make me feel better. Good people are good medicine.

Helping others is a sure way to boost your mood, too. If your social life feels lackluster, or you've been feeling lonely or isolated, get involved with your community. "Helper's high" is a real thing.

4. Choose brain-boosting foods.

Certain food choices reduce inflammation, are associated with lower rates of depression, and enhance your brain's performance (I'll share lots more about this in Chapter 10). I notice a big difference between the way I feel when I wake after a day (or a week) of eating "clean," versus how I feel after indulging in tons of carbs, sugar, and meat over a holiday weekend. After the latter, I often feel low or irritable and my body is tired. My face looks puffy, tired, and older. No thank you! I'll probably always have indulgent days or weekends, but I prefer to feel good. Most days, I try to make really positive food choices. I encourage you to do the same, especially if low moods are an issue for you.

5. Be cautious with alcohol.

I love a good glass of wine. But whenever I drink it more regularly or in larger amounts (i.e., summer or holidays), I notice a negative effect on my mood. I'm more irritable, less able to deal with stress, and more likely to get emotional. I'll start to feel blue when I wake up in the morning.

Alcohol is a known brain depressant. Increased intake over time is associated with increased incidence of depression.[5] When I drink, I eat way more food, thanks to alcohol's disinhibiting effects. It's also less healthy food, typically, than I would choose if drinking something non-alcoholic.

Not everyone gets impacted the same way. Pay close attention to how alcohol affects you, beyond the early buzz from the first few sips. Women are more sensitive to alcohol than men, and we all get more sensitive as we get older.

During high-pressure or high-performance seasons, for example, if I have a very important speech or deadline, I abstain from alcohol for a couple of weeks to a month beforehand. This optimizes my brain function, my mood, and my ability to handle stress. Figure out what rhythm or pattern works best to suit your health goals, your mental health goals, and your life.

6. Get enough sleep.

I'm going to spend an entire chapter on this later. Figure out how much sleep you need on a regular basis to feel your best. Do everything you can to make that happen. Get help from your doctor if it's a struggle. Everything is easier when you're well rested.

7. Practice gratitude as a discipline.

Years ago, I first read about the "What-Went-Well Exercise" (WWW) in *Flourish*, Martin Seligman's classic book about positive psychology and human well-being.[6] Seligman is widely acknowledged as the founder of positive psychology. According to him, "we think too much about what goes wrong and not enough about what goes right in our lives."

The official format for doing the WWW exercise goes like this: At the end of your day, write down three things that went well (aka "Three Blessings"). Next to each positive event, answer this: "Why did this happen?" (e.g., My son brought me flowers—because he's a great kid and I've raised him well). Based on Seligman's research, if you do this for just a week, "odds are that you will be less depressed, happier, and addicted to this exercise, six months from now."[6]

It works. I do a paper-free version. Every night, right before I go to sleep, I think of three good things that happened in my day. I imagine them in my mind, which recreates the good feeling. I thank God for those events as part of my bedtime prayer practice. It's amazing how even on the hardest days, the good things are there. It helps so much to see them.

I've assigned this exercise to many people, with such positive results. I once suggested it to a very intense, competitive executive who was suffering from significant burnout. I never thought he'd do it, but he did. And he said it changed his life!

I know what it's like to be vulnerable to depression and low moods. I probably have a genetic component to it, and my poor brain has been through the ringer (between med school, residency, and some of the other trials I've put it through). The evidence-based strategies and practices that I've shared here have changed my life. And they can really improve yours.

5

CALM ANXIETY, FACE YOUR FEARS, AND TAKE BACK YOUR LIFE

A few years ago, I received a coaching request from a high-ranking executive in Asia. She had just received the promotion of her dreams, at a huge multinational organization. She wanted to do her best, but feared the worst.

"Some of my old tigers are back," Annie wrote. "I constantly feel anxious, and feel weirdly insecure. Can you help me?"

In our first session, I started with the basics. Until she started this new job, she'd been sleeping seven to eight hours a night. Now, she was getting home later from work, going to bed later, and getting up earlier. She was getting six hours, if she was lucky. Here was the first clue to why she was feeling so off (in Chapter 9, I'll discuss the link between reduced sleep and anxiety).

Next, I asked about exercise. She loved to run, but hadn't in quite a while. She noted that it used to really help her burn off stress and feel less anxious. This was clue number two.

She also told me that she felt the most anxious in the mornings, on the train to work. Her thoughts would race, and her body felt like it was humming with stress and tension. We started talking about some of the things she would be worrying about, but then something occurred to me.

"Wait a minute," I said. "What are you eating for breakfast?" I asked.

"Nothing, really," she said. "I have my coffee while I'm getting the girls ready to go to school, and then I head out the door."

"Is there any milk in your coffee?" I asked.

"No, just sugar," Annie replied. Aha. Clue number three.

If I suddenly get anxious, irritable, foggy-headed, paralytically indecisive, weirdly weepy or what I might call "melty," it's often because I need to eat. In my twenties, I finally connected my melty moments to probable changes in blood sugar. I once started crying in a grocery store because I couldn't decide which protein bar to buy (talk about embarrassing). I was with a friend, who kindly suggested that maybe I needed to eat something. I picked a bar, took a bite, and felt better in a few seconds. It was a revelation. Ever since then, I always make sure that I eat throughout the day and carry high-protein snacks with me.

I imagined that some "real" food in the morning would probably be helpful in stabilizing Annie's mood and blood sugar. Some people can get away without eating breakfast, but most people feel and perform better when they eat something early in the day, even if it's just a protein-based smoothie (my breakfast of choice).

Finally, we got talking about Annie's anxious thoughts. Even though she'd been incredibly successful throughout her life, always at the top at school or work, she doubted and second-guessed herself constantly. I see this all the time, working with the most extraordinary and accomplished people. You'd never guess how many insecure and anxious thoughts go through their minds. It's such a privilege for me to have this glimpse into people's reality. It helps me a lot, too, when I have similar thoughts. It's common to be successful and still doubt yourself. It doesn't mean the doubtful thoughts are true (more on that in a bit), but it can be very reassuring to know that your self-doubt and "impostor syndrome" thoughts are very normal. Impostor syndrome, by the way, is commonly found in high achievers. It tends to be experienced by women more frequently than men, and also by college students who belong to marginalized groups.[1]

So, I encouraged Annie to wrap up her work earlier, go to bed earlier, and eat some kind of protein-rich food in the morning along with her coffee (she started eating a lower-carb protein bar, as she didn't have time to make anything). She started running again—just a little, but enough to notice the difference.

Her morning-train anxiety dropped dramatically after she started eating breakfast, and she also used that time to practice healthier thoughts. When she starting doubting her ability to succeed at her job, she stopped those thoughts and reminded herself of all her accomplishments. She repeated the words that her mentors had told her, about how exceptionally skilled and talented she is. We also discussed ways for her to let go of things that she was trying to control that she didn't need to. She stopped attending meetings that she didn't need to go to (she'd been going because she felt anxious about missing out on any discussions, but finally acknowledged that this "control" habit wasted time and energy).

I taught her the 4-6-8 breath, which she found helpful whenever she felt anxiety rising. We also discussed her top life priorities, which helped her feel more purposeful and less guilty for putting her family ahead of work. She'd been working so much that she rarely was able to tuck her girls into bed. We also discussed what she loved about her job, which helped her feel less resentful and more connected to the real meaning that it brought to her life. She reconnected with friends who believed in her and made her laugh. She also missed the faith that she'd grown up with, and started using her train time to listen to podcasts from a pastor whose teachings she really resonated with.

She described this whole process as an experience of reclaiming her "lost self." Through a combination of lack of self-care, disconnection with priorities, and inaccurate thoughts, Annie had disappeared. But now she was back. A few months into our work together, she told me: "My health is better and my self-doubt is much less. I'm able to stay in the present now. My interactions with my team and clients feel rewarding again. I'm less emotional, and I'm communicating better. More than anything, I'm less mean to myself. Life feels so much better."

My approach to anxiety is like my approach to pretty much every significant problem (including how to live a more resilient life). Focus on the fundamentals of sleep, nutrition, exercise. Look at your thoughts. Look at your life. Look at your work. Look at your world. Know your priorities. Shift what has gotten out of balance.

AN EPIDEMIC OF WORRY

If you're chronically worried, socially anxious, or prone to panic, you're not alone. Anxiety is the most common mental health disorder in the United States.[2] In Canada, anxiety disorders impacted nearly 5 percent of the entire population during pre-pandemic times,[3] and the numbers have gotten much worse since (depending on which report you read; it can be challenging to keep up with the numbers). Those are just the people with a formally diagnosed anxiety disorder. Many others may be chronically anxious, but haven't told anyone. Or their fears may not be intense enough for those feelings to qualify for a diagnosis.

The term "anxiety disorders" covers a range of conditions. Common diagnosable anxiety conditions include generalized anxiety disorder (GAD), panic disorder, obsessive-compulsive disorder (OCD), phobias, and post-traumatic stress disorder (PTSD). As a side note, PTSD has been recategorized as a "trauma and stressor-related disorder" in the latest edition of the bible of psychiatry, the *Diagnostic and Statistical Manual of Mental Disorders (DSM-5).*[4] Trauma unquestionably causes PTSD, but I still think of it as an anxiety disorder (and many experts in the field agree).[5] PTSD makes you feel intensely anxious and chronically on edge; I'll share more about my own experiences with trauma-related anxiety a little later in this chapter.

WHAT ARE THE SYMPTOMS OF ANXIETY?

You may think of anxiety as excessive worrying, but it presents in a variety of ways. Intense worry-focused thoughts and feelings are common symptoms, for sure, but anxiety also shows up as difficulty concentrating, distractibility, chronic tension, and insomnia. Physical symptoms include stomach upset, headaches, muscle tension, and other bodily manifestations of ongoing tension or fear.

I had a brief bout of intense anxiety during medical school, due to an unexpected personal loss. It started with a scary yet common symptom called "derealization." As I sat studying in the library, I suddenly felt weirdly detached from everything around me. The softly lit library air looked different, almost hazy. It was as if I was losing my connection with my surroundings and with the people quietly studying around me. I felt like an invisible spectator, observing the scene through a foggy window. This happened several times, with each episode lasting a few minutes. I worried that there was something physically wrong with me, but it turned out to be more like a mild panic attack. Until those symptoms appeared, I didn't realize how upset I was about the recent events that had happened in my life. Luckily, I knew enough to reach out for support, and I got help and relief quite quickly.

Speaking of panic, that's an anxiety disorder in its own right. Patients tell me that their panic attacks feel like they're going to faint or die. Panic can also wake people at night, seemingly out of nowhere. Nighttime panic startles you awake. You may feel inexplicably terrified, sometimes gasping for air. Obviously, if this happens to you, you should first make sure it isn't something physical. People with panic attacks often worry that the shortness of breath or tightness in the chest means that they are having a heart attack or something equally sinister. Usually it doesn't—but sometimes it does. Seek medical care immediately if it's the first time it happens to you, especially if shortness of breath or chest discomfort persists, or you are older or have risk factors for cardiovascular disease.

OCD is something people joke about, as in "I'm so OCD, just look at my color-coordinated closet." Obsessive compulsive disorder is not excessively tidiness, actually, and a significant number of people have OCD without being aware of it. In my work with patients, I picked up a surprising number of cases. The individual would think that they were just "too anxious" or uptight, but my questions revealed patterns that pointed to OCD. One person might have a chronic, unreasonable fear that their family will get in an accident (an "obsession," presuming it's not PTSD-related), or they might have a ritual where they feel they have to check the oven five times before going to bed, to keep their family safe (a "compulsion").

People feel powerless over these unreasonable or irrational thoughts and behaviors. They may feel ashamed and try to hide them from others. In my experience, it's a huge relief when someone finally has an explanation and a name for it all. I've also found that it's quite treatable. In many cases, talking with patients about the root sources of the anxiety, correcting distorted thinking, and setting goals around thought and behavior modification were very effective in shifting these patterns. Self-care helps, too. Medication can also be helpful in more severe cases. The biggest step, usually, is acknowledging that it's a problem, and that you're ready to do something about it.

SHOULD I BE WORRIED ABOUT HOW ANXIOUS I AM?

Worrying is normal. There are plenty of anxiety-provoking things that happen in life. Worrying, anxieties, or anxiety-driven behaviors become problematic when they've been happening for a prolonged time, take over your daily life, affect your functioning at work/school/home, or impact your relationships.

If you look at the DSM-5 diagnostic criteria for GAD,[6] there are several key features:

- Excessive anxiety and worry, or apprehensive expectation, occurring more days than not for at least 6 months, about a number of events or activities (such as work or school performance)

- The person finds it difficult to control the worry

- The anxiety and worry are associated with three or more of the following: restlessness or feeling keyed up or on edge; being easily fatigued; difficulty concentrating; irritability; muscle tension; sleep disturbance

As always, please don't diagnose yourself, but this illustrates what problematic anxiety looks like. If your worries are causing you significant distress, you should talk to a professional. And again, talk to your doctor first, as there are medical conditions that mimic anxiety disorders, like an overactive thyroid gland.

HEALING ANXIETY BY RETRAINING YOUR BRAIN

In Chapter 1, I talked about the miracle of neuroplasticity—the brain's ability to change and adapt to fresh information or stimuli. I shared how I love to use this to encourage patients with anxiety. It would take a whole book—or much more, really—to get into all the neuroscience, but I want to share with you some basics here.

I wouldn't describe myself as anxious now. In the past, though, in addition to the brief spell of panic I described earlier, I developed a mild form of what some experts might call "complex" post-traumatic stress symptoms. This type of trauma syndrome results from a series of intensely difficult or frightening events or situations, often over the course of years, rather than a single traumatizing event. I'd get triggered by certain situations, or certain things related to those situations. In highly stressful seasons of my life, usually when I was in a particularly difficult and prolonged situation, my anxiety would ramp way up. Sometimes, after the situation was over and the active threat was gone, I would still feel keyed up, on edge, and reactive.

On a biological or neurological level, the fear center of my brain (the limbic system, a major player of which is the amygdala) hadn't clued in that the threat was gone. The experience of that situation had been so stressful for my brain that it was afraid to let its guard down. It decided to continually protect itself from any potential future threats. Even if there really weren't any.

Thankfully, one day I had a chance encounter with a trauma expert at a medical conference. We sat next to each other at lunch and got to chatting. When she mentioned her field of expertise, I made some brief references to some of the things I'd experienced. She looked at me intently and said, "You should probably get help with that." I ended up booking a few sessions with her, and she recommended EMDR (Eye Movement Desensitization and Reprocessing Treatment). This trauma-specific therapy, which helps the brain reintegrate traumatic memories, helped me a lot, as did some of the strategies that I'm about to discuss. When the brain gets stuck in anxious patterns, neuroscience-based strategies can bring both the brain and body back to a calmer, more grounded baseline.

I want to emphasize again that this is not a complete discussion of trauma or a prescription for the treatment of trauma. Trauma is a very delicate and complex subject, in which I am not an expert. I share my story and perspective as an illustration of one person's experience, a person who also happens to be a physician. If you have significant symptoms of trauma, get qualified expert help. Please filter anything I say here through your qualified trauma professional before implementing anything.

IF YOU LET ANXIETY RUN YOUR SHOW, IT GETS STRONGER

Once we've locked in a fear response in our brain, it resists new information and wants to reinforce that fear circuit. I've heard experts liken the limbic system or amygdala to a small fearful child. A child that is very difficult to convince of the truth.

Let's say you've become anxious about going to dinner parties. It started when someone made fun of you at a friend's birthday dinner.

And then it happened again, another time. You felt so embarrassed that you decided you wouldn't go to dinner parties anymore. It's been over a year and you've realized, more and more, that you're missing out on a lot.

Someone asks you to go to a party tonight. You don't want to miss out anymore, so you say yes. You get dressed up. As you get into your car, though, fear kicks in. Your heart races. You feel wound up and uncomfortable. What if something awful happens again? It doesn't feel safe. Maybe it's a terrible idea.

The only way to guarantee a good outcome is to stay home. You text your friend with an excuse. Instantly, you feel the anxiety go away. You're a little embarrassed about canceling, but more than anything, you feel safe. Your heart has calmed down.

Here's what happened in your brain, though. Your limbic system alerted you to "danger" with the possibility of going to the party. When you paid attention to the fear signals and stress response generated by your limbic system in response to the "trigger" (going to the party), and decided not to go, guess what? You reinforced the programming in your brain that parties are "dangerous" and should be avoided to keep you safe. Your anxiety reaction, the next time you try to go, may be even stronger.

You can heal and retrain this entrenched system in your brain by giving the limbic system new information. Ideally you would do this with the help of a counselor, but if the symptoms are relatively mild, you may decide to try this on your own. The following concepts have been really useful to me and the patients and clients that I have worked with.

1. Start small and be brave.
If there's something you're avoiding, and your anxiety around it is getting worse, set yourself up for small wins. Be brave. It will show that "little child" in your brain's fear center that the "unsafe" assessment isn't accurate, that that position needs to change. By the way, though it may sound like it, I'm not just talking about phobias here (and if you do have a specific phobia, please work it through with a professional). This

also works for everyday anxiety-provoking situations in which avoidance can become a habit.

Whether you've stopped going to social events or are avoiding something else that you long to do, pick an easy win to start with. The fear will probably kick up, but if you can get past it, your brain will have a new data point. Commit to doing whatever it is, and to not letting the fear stop you. Enjoy yourself as you're doing that thing, when you get to the other side of your fear. Pay attention to all the good feelings that come from overcoming your fears and enjoying your life. It's time to reeducate your brain that parties—or whatever it is for you—are fun, really quite safe, and well worth whatever small risk might be involved.

2. Acknowledge the fear, but put it in perspective.

When fear comes up, take a step back. Once you understand that this is just your brain responding to a trigger, you can observe it more objectively versus letting the fear response overwhelm your rational mind.

You can say something to yourself like "This is just my fear system talking; this isn't really me," or "My limbic system thinks this party is a threat, but it's wrong—I like these friends and I want to go." Or, "This feels scary, but I know that I need to do this in order to help my brain heal and to enjoy my life again." Take a breath to calm your system. Get really rational and practical. And again—really celebrate the triumph, and pat yourself on the back, for being brave and conquering your fears. For not letting them hold you back anymore.

3. Shift a fear pattern by directing your attention to good things (or anything else, really).

I used this approach with a road that I used to get really freaked out about. I had a bad experience once, driving a terrifying stretch of highway in the Mexican Baja. It was a high, steep, winding mountain road with no guardrails and no visibility around corners. The desert far below was littered with cars that hadn't made it. I didn't have an accident, but had a couple of close calls around blind corners. I've struggled with high mountain roads ever since.

On road trips in my local area, I often have to drive through another steep, twisting desert road. It's much safer and has enormous guardrails, but it would still trigger me. If my husband was driving, I'd sink down so low that I'd practically be under the dash, eyes tight shut and praying out loud. If I was driving, I'd go so slowly that I'd almost come to a stop while inching around corners. A bit excessive, but try to tell that to my amygdala. It had learned that high mountain roads could be fatal, and it wanted to protect me. My amygdala had no idea that I was actually safe, nor did I.

I eventually had enough of this and decided to apply some neuroscience principles to the situation. I needed to teach my brain to have a different response. So, I decided to intensely focus on what was good. This "safe" high road overlooks a beautiful lake. It was hard at first, but I forced myself to stay upright as the car descended, and take in the beautiful view. I found different aspects of the view to focus on. I would even say aloud, with deliberate delight, "Isn't this place so gorgeous?"

My amygdala got the message surprisingly quickly. These days, I sometimes make it through that crazy set of hairpins without even remembering that I used to be terrified. I used to anticipate every single curving corner with terror and tension. Now, if I get caught up in the sunny day or a happy song, I might arrive at the bottom without even noticing I'd come down the hill. In the rare event that the anxiety tries to come back, I just redirect my attention to the beautiful view and everything calms down.

Back to the example of the party. If you get yourself there (bravo!), intentionally focus on what's joyful and good. Look around at the beloved faces of your friends. Really taste the delicious food. Savor the laughter. Let your heart feel the love of good people who you really enjoy being with. Feel the safety. Let that get into your bones. It will get into your brain, too, and will start to change (and heal) your limbic system's erroneous narrative around parties—and anything else you might be irrationally or habitually afraid of.

4. Live a calm and calming life.

If you're in a season where you're feeling anxious, whether it's a "clinical" degree of anxiety or not, be kind and gentle with yourself. Don't force yourself to do things that have nothing to do with the source of your anxiety but make you feel more stressed.

I won't watch really scary, dark, or violent movies, as a general rule. I've worked in an ER. I've been in some profoundly difficult situations. I've experienced enough stress, tension, and other awful things. I don't need that in my entertainment.

Practice mindfulness, or other mind-body techniques that calm your nervous system down and feel soothing. Remember to breathe, especially if you're stressed. If there are people in your life that you find really stressful, who you don't have to see on a regular basis, maybe you don't need to see them in this season.

Spend time in nature. Take a vacation, if you can, even if it's just a staycation. Nourish yourself with beautiful, healthy foods. Listen to music that feels healing and calming. Go for walks. Sit by the water. Drink cozy herbal tea. Cuddle with your pet or your honey. If you have a hard time taking good care of yourself, remind yourself that at a time like this, such things aren't luxuries—they're essential.

5. Rewire your brain with truth.

In my experience, both personally and when practicing cognitive behavioral therapy with patients, it's so helpful to think of your brain as a machine that can stuck in a pattern of error that needs to be rewired. As in Annie's case, anxious people usually have thought distortions. Maybe you keep thinking that "something always goes wrong for me." Maybe there's some truth to that. Maybe you've had some really raw deals. I get it. I've been there. But I bet it's not true all the time. It's probably not true most of the time.

What's the truth?

Let's say that you want to embark on a project that you're really excited about. You're qualified; you've got the experience. It's a novel idea but you think it's a good one. You've shared your idea with a couple of mentors, and they've been encouraging. Yet that thought holds you back: "Something could go wrong, and that would be disastrous. It would really be safer not to try, so maybe you shouldn't." Really?

What's the truth?

I talk this question through with people, or assign homework around it. It can be very useful to write down a fearful thought that's holding you back or making your life miserable. Next, take that thought and apply these questions (we'll do this as a Coaching Exercise in a moment):

Where did that fear come from?

What's true about it?

What's not true about it?

What is the real probability that something will go wrong in this particular scenario? Will you regret it if you don't give it a try?

What are the probable negative outcomes or losses you might experience if you give into the fear again?

What are the probable positive outcomes if you step past your fear and move forward?

Usually, the answer is clear. When looked at in the light of reason and objective facts, this is a reasonable "risk" to take. So, you take it (and continue to talk to a counselor, mentor, or friend, or your journal, as fears come up). Feel that fear. Feel all the fears. Do that thing anyway.

COACHING EXERCISE

Is there something you're frequently anxious about?

Is there a specific thought or belief related to it?

Write it down, and then go through the above list of questions, writing your answers.

What is the truth?

How might this change what you decide to do going forward?

*6. If you're worrying a lot about something,
designate a focused time for that.*
If there's something that's constantly on your mind, don't let that ruin your day or run your mind. It can be helpful to designate a set time every day to think about and even write out your concerns (see the next tip). At that specific time, you can let yourself feel how upset you are and problem-solve potential worst-case scenarios. The rest of the time, if you catch yourself beginning to worry and obsess, stop yourself and save your concerns for your designated time the next day.

When you become determined not to let anxious thoughts take over your mind, you're helping your brain shift from a chronically anxious kind of "wiring" to a more balanced, healthy new normal. You can literally shift the habitual paths that your mind and brain take, and create new, healthier ones. The less you let your mind worry, the less your brain will spontaneously generate anxious thoughts. The more you focus on what's true and good, the more you'll naturally focus on those things. Your brain shifts its patterns accordingly. It's a beautiful thing.

7. Try expressive writing.
Expressive writing, or writing about difficult emotions that you have about your life or a specific situation, has been found to be beneficial in a wide range of studies. You could set a fixed amount of time, each day, to write out how you feel about difficult things that are going on. This has been shown to help with mild to moderate depression and anxiety, and even improves symptoms of chronic pain. (It may not be helpful immediately after a significantly traumatic event, though; experts recommend waiting a month or two for things to settle before using this in that circumstance. Again, only attempt this with the guidance of a professional if you've experienced significant trauma.)

This can be very helpful to do before bed if you suffer from the kind of insomnia where anxious thoughts keep you up at night. It can even help you perform better at work-related tasks that you find anxiety-provoking.

Finally, as I discussed with Annie, there are some very basic things you can do if you've been feeling unusually anxious:

- Reduce caffeine intake.

If you're feeling keyed up all day and having trouble falling asleep, consider reducing your caffeine intake. Gradually stop all sources of caffeine, including chocolate, and see if it helps.

- Take better care of yourself.

If you, like Annie, are sleeping less than six hours a night, you're probably looking at a prime cause of your anxiety. True, anxiety can make it hard to sleep, but if you can get eight hours of sleep, you should notice an immediate difference in your mood. Exercise is also fantastic for healing an anxious brain and discharging physical tension from worries; try to get twenty to thirty minutes of cardiovascular exercise every day. Finally, eat good food. Start your day with something of substance. In general, aim to minimize processed foods, alcohol, and sugar, and eat a rich variety of healthy whole foods. Our brains are very sensitive to the kinds of fuel we give them, and good food goes a long, long way (more on this in Chapter 10).

- Get help.

If your anxiety is significantly impacting your life and relationships, I will say it again: don't try to white-knuckle this on your own. See your doctor to assess whether your anxiety might have a medical cause. If it seems to be purely psychological, expert counseling treatments such as CBT can be extremely helpful here, too.

As you can tell, I'm a proponent of trying non-pharmaceutical treatments first. Still, medication can be a lifesaver if you're drowning and can't function in your daily life. I often tell people that it's unlikely that they'll be on medication for the rest of their lives, particularly if they take steps to get support and address the underlying causes of anxiety. For many, an appropriately selected, evidence-based, non-addictive medication can take the edge off during a season of crisis. It helps immensely when you're no longer just trying to survive your days, and can take the necessary steps to get your life back on track.

I know that some of this may seem eye-rollingly simplistic, especially if you're having a really difficult time. I assure you, though, that the principles underlying these strategies are sound. These tactics have worked wonders for me, in additional to receiving expert counseling and support. I feel so much calmer now than I used to.

Again, some anxieties, especially if related to trauma, require a multi-pronged and specialized approach to treatment. And again, you may benefit from taking medication for a time period. Still, you'd be surprised by how helpful it can be to understand your brain and its relationship to the anxiety you feel, and the simple things you can do to take back control—versus letting irrational anxieties run your show and your brain.

As an end note, there is a profound truth about life that illustrates something important about anxiety. Most things in life that are worth doing, that will stretch you and bring you closer to your goals and dreams, will feel intensely uncomfortable. It helps so much to understand and embrace the fact that fear accompanies change. Fear accompanies so many good changes. Just because you feel afraid or anxious, it doesn't mean that something is bad or that something bad will happen. If you're facing something that you want to do and it scares you, get used to the discomfort. Get used to how it feels to move forward while feeling uncomfortable or even breathlessly apprehensive.

Avoid the mistake of thinking that because you're afraid, you shouldn't do it. Often, fear actually means that you're on the right track. You can do this.

6

WHAT TO DO WHEN CRISIS (INEVITABLY) HITS

My immigrant parents, who moved to North America from Europe and the Middle East, taught me to work hard and be tough. Whenever things get really difficult, I keep going as a way of coping. I'll even crank my efforts (and standards) higher. Overall, this has served me well. It has made me a fiercely independent woman. I've always been able to provide for myself and get through crises without too much collateral damage. Unfortunately, this ability to keep my head up and soldier on also produced spinoff effects that became problematic later on.

My first year of medical school was pretty brutal. A lot of upsetting, challenging things happened, some too private to share here. I faced multiple personal and health crises, including a bout with a probable mononucleosis infection, that put me in bed for a stretch of time (the mono was probably the easiest of the hard things). I just kept going.

My class schedule was packed with endless lectures and enormous amounts of learning material. I remember staying home sick in bed and feeling so exhausted that it took effort to sit up. My friends came by every evening with a thick pile of notes from the day's lectures. I'd force myself to read them and memorize them.

Despite all the things that happened that chaotic and painful year, I never allowed myself to lose focus. I was shocked, at the end of the academic year, to receive a letter congratulating me on being the top student in the entire class. I had just been trying to keep up; I never realized that I had been excelling.

I think of that determined, resilient girl now, and marvel at her grit. It amazes me that she accomplished this, during *that* year. Now, it's important to recognize that my success was largely a result of being so well resourced (a.k.a. privileged). I come from a stable family background, got an excellent education, lived in a safe home and neighborhood, had good friends, accessed free health care, went to a good university, received scholarships and bursaries that paid for tuition, rent, and food, and so on. Still, it amazes me that I was psychologically able to keep going like I did, month after long month.

I also feel so much compassion for that plucky girl. More than anything, what she needed during that season was way more love and support—and better treatment from certain key people, who made that year much harder than it needed to be.

So, the way that I naturally cope with crises is through sheer will and icy determination. I shove my feelings down and focus on what needs to get done. That's useful when a crisis requires a decisive, unemotional response or plan of action, but it's a terrible way to live long term. As part of my "keep going at all costs" pattern, I also ignored or glossed over inconvenient information or bad behavior in relationships. Everything's fine—really, it is (when it's so not).

We're not machines. You can't shove down your emotions and

ignore your legitimate needs forever. Cracks form. Things start to spill out. Things explode.

Even though I liked to think I was fine, my behavior with food showed me that I wasn't. For years, rather than calling out bad behavior, or properly dealing with a situation, I would eat cookies and ice cream and, very specifically, carrot cake. I would go to a nearby grocery store and buy an entire cake, to be consumed that night.

I also acted like a "drama queen" at inopportune moments, when I just couldn't hold things in anymore. Yelling would diffuse some of that pent-up emotion, but it wouldn't actually solve problems and would just make me look bad or unbalanced. Sigh.

I'm happy to report, though, that I got wiser and more mature as the years went by. By the time I went through a really difficult season a few years ago, I finally hit escape velocity. My will and determination took on a new form. I was not going to let an unjust situation take me down. But this time, I was going to take the best care of myself, and my life, that I could. No more white-knuckling through on my own. No more shoving things down. I was going to get through this one whole. I was going to come out stronger and better. And I really did.

From a lot of experience, here are the things that I recommend you keep top of mind, and do, when crisis hits:

1. Let the people around you give to you, help you, and support you.
"Strong" people like me can be really proud—too proud and independent to ask for and receive help. During that more recent difficult season, I uncharacteristically embraced and leaned on the people around me. A new, very wise friend (who is also a counselor) would invite me over and let me vent for hours. To this day, years later, she still calls to see if I need a good long chat about anything. Another good friend, who was going through a similar situation in her life, met with me every week for dinner. We would laugh to the point of tears at some of the things we were having to deal with.

An eighty-year-old friend offered to temporarily house my dog until

I was able to find a rental that allowed pets. I looked up and joined a small neighborhood group at my new church, where wonderful strangers gathered around me and supported me. They are still some of my closest friends. I also met with a couple of counselors who I had seen in the past, who reassured me that I was still mentally healthy and wasn't losing my mind, even though it felt like it some days. They encouraged and helped me so much in moving forward and taking good care of myself.

Recall Michael Ungar's statement: "If one wants to be strong during a crisis, it's best to invest in others before the crisis occurs."[1] As I'll discuss in Chapter 7, it's important to invest in connections with good people, as a key focus of your life. And when times get rough, don't hesitate to reach out to friends and family, as well as new social connections or community resources, for help and support.

2. Protect your means to earn a living.

When I was younger and full of exuberance about all the possibilities that life could hold, I encouraged people to drop everything and follow their dreams. In a way, I had done so for a time, when I moved my base to Mexico for several years, to focus on dancing and writing. A pretty wild move for a medical doctor. Many people questioned and criticized it.

My practical, immigrant roots held fast, though. My dad thought I should open my own medical clinic and was upset about the move (at one point, hammering his fist on the kitchen table as he shouted: "When will you realize that life isn't supposed to be fun?!"). I wasn't about to take his advice, but I wasn't going to be foolish, either. I made sure I had a backup plan.

I have earned income from things other than clinical medicine for a long time now, and could easily have stopped practicing medicine. I was very careful, nonetheless, to keep that medical license valid and up to date. I made sure I worked whatever clinical hours were required to maintain it, and took continuing education courses and so on. Sure enough, in certain difficult seasons (such as the 2008 crash, when multiple sources of my non-clinical revenue dried up), I was very glad to still have it.

Obviously, not everyone has a medical license to lean on in hard times. I know I'm extremely privileged. But I now advise young people to try to have a stable, reliable way to make income in difficult times, no matter what their dreams may be.

When crisis or tragedy broadsides your life, protect your work or your livelihood. When things are going well, nurture your work, your skills, your qualifications, and your ability to make an income carefully, so that it's all there for you when things go sideways. Yes, sometimes circumstances are so difficult that you must take time off (or maybe lose your job), but keep working if you can, even if it's really hard. Show up and do good work. Be responsible and reliable. Protecting your work can be the thing that gets you through a crisis, psychologically and financially.

I also recommend that you proactively protect your financial health, and your ability to weather a crisis or disaster, by having appropriate insurance coverage, keeping your legal affairs in order, minimizing or eliminating debt, and building savings, if possible, such as a six-month emergency fund.

3. Draw strength from structure.

I've talked about how structure in your life makes you more resilient. I shared how my preestablished schedule and my old and new respon- sibilities got me out of bed and kept me going during the extremely difficult season of my husband's accident. Michael Ungar points out that "rules, routines and expectations make our lives predictable and secure." He notes that job security, which I emphasized in the last section, helps us weather challenges, and that "our need for structure increases in times of crisis."[1]

When life sends you spinning, it's natural to want to chop away at your life and your responsibilities, to create space to deal with or emo- tionally process the crisis. And for sure, there are times for that. When someone close to us dies, we benefit from a short period where all we need to do is mourn and recover from the shock of the loss. I took that stress leave from the ER when my burnout and depression had reached a crisis point. As a rule, though, don't dismantle the structure of your life. Keep showing up and doing what you can, while simultaneously taking care of your needs. That structure is precious psychological and physical scaffolding that you need in difficult times.

4. Make choices that will make your life better,
not worse, when the dust settles.

When things are really bad, you can easily justify "unhelpful" choices. Who wouldn't be driven to drink? Would anyone blame you for living off of ice cream, chocolate, and cigarettes? Same goes for signing up for that dating (hookup?) app to distract yourself from a devastating breakup.

Bad ideas. Really bad ideas. All of them.

One of the best lessons I learned, from the various unwanted crises I have experienced, is that you should fight back against the terrible blows or events that life hands out, by being ferociously committed to caring for yourself in those times. Be determined, with everything that's in you, to not do things that you'll regret. There are lots of things that might feel good or provide relief in the moment, but will cause your life to spiral further down.

This mindset provides you with an enormous reservoir of strength. There are times when I've felt so upset by something that has happened that I'm tempted to just melt into despair. For a moment, I want to give up. In the old days, there would have been a lot of carrot cake involved, and other unhelpful coping "strategies."

Today, I let myself feel and process the pain constructively. I don't waste time yelling at someone who doesn't really care or won't change. I vent to God instead (which I find really helpful). I get counseling support. I journal. I read helpful articles online. I lean on my friends. And in those moments where I'm tempted to do something that will be ultimately harmful to me (like a sugar binge, or drinking alone), I ask myself this: *What would be the most useful thing, for myself and my life, that I could do right now?*

There are only good answers to this question. Maybe I need to go for a brisk, angry walk. Or call a friend. Or vigorously scrub the dishes (I find cleaning and creating order to be enormously therapeutic). Maybe I'll finally sort through those receipts and get caught up on my finances.

I cannot put into words how good it feels when something terrible happens to you and you choose to do something healthy, positive, or constructive with your negative energy. High-five yourself mentally when you do it. You go. You rock. You've got this.

If you, like me in the past, have habitually turned to unhelpful coping strategies that you regret, make this the day that you commit to ferociously, brilliantly caring for yourself (and the ones you love) in the midst of any crisis.

5. Look after your health.
As an absolute priority, make time for the key building blocks of physical health and well-being in tough times. Make them the foundation of your days, as hard as it may be. Get enough sleep. Choose nutritious foods. Make sure you have healthy food in your house and eat three good meals a day. If you have to eat out, make it something healthy that vitalizes you. Even fast-food places have "better" choices on their menu—choose those. Say no to fries on the side and make it a salad instead. Drink lots of water. Go for walks, or exercise in other ways. These life-giving choices, made as often as possible, will help you be restored, well-fueled, destressed, energized, and far more able to deal with whatever it is you have to navigate. I'll share more motivating information, along with lots of tips and strategies, in the chapters on sleep, nutrition, and exercise.

6. Count your blessings, literally.
In the early days of that hard season, I found myself invited to the dinner table of a kind pastor and his wife. After listening to all that

was happening in my life, she turned to me with a gentle smile and said: "Once, when I went through a really terrible time, someone told me to carry a little book with me. She said that even on the worst days, I should watch for small miracles. Every time something unexpectedly positive happened, I was to write it down. By the time I got through that season, that little book was filled with so many good things that I lost count. I still go back and look at that amazing little book, years later."

The next day, I bought a tiny, beautiful book to carry in my purse. Virtually every day, there was something, or several things, to write down. During moments of despair while driving somewhere, songs would come on the radio that seemed like they were written for me, for that very moment. On a gloomy day, while walking outside (because I knew it was good for me), the clouds suddenly parted and the sun beamed down on my face. Its warmth followed me for the rest of my walk. There were so many small moments like these. They made a difference, and made me feel less alone with my pain.

Some of the things that happened were truly extraordinary. Someone I had briefly met at a trade show a few years prior emailed me about a virtual medicine clinic he was opening. When I'd met him, he was involved in another, totally unrelated field. We had chatted for a couple of minutes and exchanged cards. When he contacted me, I had taken a break from practicing medicine but was planning to pick it up again shortly.

I was curious about the new clinic, so I called him. He offered me a job on the spot. I would be able to practice medicine from home and completely design my own schedule. I could see patients for a couple of hours here, a couple of hours there, whatever I wished. I felt stunned that such a job even existed. This happened years before the COVID-19 pandemic, before virtual medicine became commonplace. It felt like a gift, and I shed a few tears of gratitude and awe. It was incredible to have this kind of control over my schedule, and to not have to commute to my usual intense medical shifts, during this grief-filled season.

I encourage you to keep track of your blessings during difficult times, whether it's in a physical notebook or a notes app on your phone.

Actively watch out for and expect the good, whenever you're going through something bad. Later, share what you discovered with others. Encourage them with your stories about the surprising goodness of life in dark times, when they are in their nightmare season.

A final note: You may have noticed periodic faith-related comments in my stories and other references to church, prayer, and so on. I've deliberately held back from sharing any more than that about my personal faith perspective (I'm Christian, though I wasn't yet in some of the stories I've shared). This book is written for you. I don't know what your background or belief system is, and I want to intentionally respect that and not superimpose my own beliefs. That said, I don't think I can honestly discuss resilience, and especially resilience in a crisis, without sharing that my specific faith, my faith community, and spiritual practices such as prayer (and the prayers of others) feel as essential to me as sleep, nutrition, and exercise, in helping me get through difficult times today.

***

I hope that your life today is stable, that all is going well, and that you already incorporate the key resilience-building, crisis-weathering factors that I described here. If not, and you are reading this at a really difficult time, I hope you can hear me cheering for you and encouraging you.

Let the people around you, and your community, help and support you. Do whatever you can to protect your work and your financial health. Draw strength from, and hang on to, the structure and responsibilities in your life. Be ferociously protective of yourself, your health, and what matters most. Make good choices that you'll be proud of. And count those blessings. Watch for them every day.

COACHING EXERCISE

Take an inventory of your life today.

Go through the list of points and ask yourself whether you can strengthen yourself by enhancing your use of, or your well-being related to, each of these areas (put a star beside any areas you would like to work on):

- *Building a strong network and letting people support and help you*

- *Protecting your work, your ability to make a living, and your financial health*

- *Having positive structure and routines in your life*

- *Making good choices when you're upset or things are difficult*

- *Caring for the basics of your health (sleep, nutrition, exercise)*

- *Counting your blessings*

For each area you have starred (and it can just be one), write down a specific action that you can take to begin strengthening this (or each) area. Put it on your calendar, and do it.

PART IV

STRENGTHEN YOUR LIFE THROUGH HEALTHY RELATIONSHIPS

7

RECLAIMING COMMUNITY IN AN ISOLATING WORLD

For several years, I ran a year-long coaching program that brought together women from around the world, from a variety of cultures and backgrounds. One of the modules was about building and strengthening healthy relationships, and I received the same question from multiple participants.

"What should I do," each person asked, "if I have a friend who rarely reaches out to me? I feel like I'm always the one who is texting or calling, and suggesting we get together. I'm tired of how imbalanced it feels. Should I give up on the friendship?"

This question affected me on a personal level. I'm highly introverted, so I'm one of those quiet friends. I get caught up in my little world. I feel so content with my books, my work, long walks with my dog, and my home life. I love my friends, but doing something social isn't always top of mind. Thank goodness for my gregarious, extraverted friends who persistently reach out and remind me of the world beyond my door. I am always glad to hear from them, love spending time with them, and am so grateful for their nudges and invitations.

My response to this question focused on the quality of the relationship. If the less communicative person was enjoyable to be around, responded positively to attempts to connect, and was otherwise a good friend, the wisest thing to do would be to keep the friendship. If you know that your friend is either really busy, or really introverted, try to stop feeling offended and keep reaching out. Good people are like gold.

As for introverted me over here, I don't get let entirely off the hook. Even though I sometimes *feel* like I don't need more people in my days, I still do.

CONNECTIONS IMPROVE YOUR LIFE, AND YOUR DAY

Tom Rath led Gallup's strengths, employee engagement, well-being, and leadership consulting for thirteen years, along with Dr. Jim Harter, PhD, Gallup's Chief Scientist of Workplace Management and Wellbeing. Their research revealed that "when we get at least six hours a day of daily social time, it increases our well-being and minimizes stress and worry."[1] In fact, each hour of social time quickly reduces the chances of having a bad day. According to Rath and Harter, just three hours of social connection reduce the chances of having a bad day to just 10 percent. On top of that, they also cite a large study of more than fifteen thousand people over the age of fifty, which found that socially active people's memories declined at less than half the rate compared to those who were the least social.

If you're an introvert like me, there's no need to panic. Daily social time includes time at work, time at home, time on the phone, and time spent on other communications like emails and texts. Face-to-face time is the best, though—we all need that in our lives. Don't tell yourself that electronic means of communication can replace real time with others.

That said, situations such as lockdowns related to COVID-19

may have inspired (or forced) you to come up with new ways of connecting or staying connected. You may want to continue these ways if they worked well and added more joy and connection to your life. My immediate family members live many miles apart, but try to come together for the holidays or special family trips. After a frustrating and lonely 2020, in which we didn't see each other nearly enough, my sister took the initiative to organize online family birthday parties, complete with hilarious games. Everyone kept commenting, "Why have we never done this before?" We're going to keep doing it.

I've embraced that if I want to feel my best and be my best, I have to push myself to be more social than I naturally want to be. These days I initiate text threads, check in with people, and invite people out, a lot more than I used to. And it's true—I do seem to be having more good days than ever before.

RELATIONSHIPS ARE EVERYTHING. FOR REAL.

The Harvard Study of Adult Development is the longest-running longitudinal study of adult life ever conducted.[2] They've studied hundreds of people's lives, from intimate medical and health details to their marriages and careers. The most startling result? Close relationships, more than money or fame, are what keep people happy throughout their lives. According to a *Harvard Gazette* report on the findings, "relationship ties protect people from life's discontents, help delay mental and physical decline, and are better predictors of long and happy lives than social class, IQ or even genes."[3]

Of course, relationships need to be healthy in order to have a healthy impact on our lives. In the next chapter, I'll cover the subject of boundaries (in both relationships and work).

MAKE PEOPLE YOUR PRIORITY

Everyone pretty much agrees that our society is the most work-obsessed in the history of humankind. Not too long ago, a person's identity came from their extended family identity, not their work. It's still that way in an ever-diminishing group of cultures in this world.

It's so easy to get sucked into our work-is-everything culture. It's especially tempting for people who passionately love their work, like I do. I (regretfully) don't have children, so that makes it even more natural for me to find my identity in work and devote my best time and energy to it.

As in so many other areas of life, we need to push against the current. We must resist the default pull, and choose what's most important to our well-being and the well-being of our society. We need to make people our priority.

You might recall my cross-country ski accident story in the introduction. I fell in the middle of a large snowy forest. My skiing companions walked me, and carried my equipment, out to safety. That happened in March, toward the end of the ski season. Almost every Saturday that winter, I had met those friends at the ski area, first thing in the morning.

Previously, I would have never done this in my life. I am not a morning person. I work hard during the week, and normally wouldn't promise Saturday mornings to anyone. But after the first couple of times I was invited out to ski with this crew, I experienced a strange rush of energy and joy that lasted the rest of the day. I'm obsessed with the research on well-being, so I realized quite quickly why I was feeling that way. It wasn't just the exercise. It wasn't just the beautiful snowscapes and fresh air. I loved skiing on my own, and felt great afterward, too. But this was different.

The magic ingredient was the friendship, connection, and laughter. It felt so powerfully good that I decided to give up the freedom of my Saturdays to experience this community on a regular basis. I could not have made better use of my time. And I, the notorious introvert recluse, started texting my friends on Friday nights if I hadn't heard anything yet about plans for Saturday morning.

If the demands of the world, or your aspirations for your career or business, threaten to isolate you from the people you love and your community, push back. Remind yourself, at the end of the day, that the people in your life are your greatest wealth. At the end of our lives, they will be what mattered most. I don't—and I'm sure you don't—want to regret not spending more time with them.

COACHING EXERCISE
Boost your resilience by taking a social inventory.

1. How is the health of your social life? Score it from 0 (terrible) to 5 (amazing).

2. Ask yourself what you need more of in your social life. Write those things down. Some examples:

   a. More time with your partner or spouse

   b. More time with friends who make you laugh

   c. More time one on one with a close friend

   d. More time going out on adventures with your kids (or anyone else you like to have fun with)

   e. More time reaching out to distant friends and relatives who you love

   f. More regular, planned activities with others, such as belonging to a team, where you'll show up and will have to go on a regular basis

3. Are there social activities you are involved in that you don't feel connected to, that don't bring you joy, and that are stealing time away from more important relationships? List them. Think about how you might shift them out of your life and calendar.

4. Take one of the types of connections from #2 that you can easily add to your life, and plan it into the next week if you can. Put it on your calendar.

5. Do it, and pay close attention to how good it made you feel.

6. Plan to do it again! Or pick something else from #2 and plan that instead.

8

PRACTICE HEALTHY BOUNDARIES AT WORK AND IN LIFE

Ignoring an offense is fine, and even laudable, in superficial and fleeting relationships. But don't be too quick to overlook bad behavior when it comes to who you let into your inner circle. We must allow people to show us who they are, rather than changing the narrative to make them into who we wish they were.

Like many people with poor boundaries, I'd learned early in life to second-guess my natural instincts about people, and to suppress appropriate negative reactions. I'd absorbed that how I felt about something or someone didn't matter as much as being nice, not being "difficult," and keeping the vibe pleasant.

This topic is very complex. The origins of unhealthy boundary habits are exceedingly complex and are of a scope that is broader than what I will cover here. If, in the past, I had been clearer about my boundaries, I would have avoided some of the greatest stress in my life. I am happy to say (and have been told) that I seem to have come through all this with resilience and better street-smarts. Still, it all took a toll on my well-being, time, energy, and resources. If I can help you make better decisions about personal and work-related relationships and situations, what I've learned will feel even more worthwhile.

DON'T TRY TO REASON WITH UNREASONABLE PEOPLE

At one point, I worked with a counselor/coach who helps women navigate and recover from unusually difficult relationships. She taught me concepts and skills that were unbelievably helpful and that translated to all kinds of relational situations. I became much better at setting boundaries (though I'm still far from perfect!). When working with coaching clients who were struggling with difficult personal or work relationships, I shared with them some of the specific strategies I learned, and watched their lives improve.

These approaches seemed so game-changing for dealing with difficult people that I decided to write about them. I titled the article "Don't Try to Reason with Unreasonable People," and posted it on my *Psychology Today* blog. To date, it's my most popular post of all time. If you need help managing your boundaries with challenging individuals, whether it's a divisive family member or a difficult boss, you're clearly not alone.

These skills can help you feel more control in these situations, and decrease the negative impact on you and on the relationship. As always, though, if you're involved in a difficult relationship, I recommend that you first speak with a counselor who understands your context, before implementing any of these strategies. That's particularly true if you're in an abusive situation, as your safety is the most important thing (more on that in a moment).

Also, when I describe people as "difficult" or "unreasonable," this doesn't mean that I'm writing them off as human beings. Some people can be difficult or unreasonable on occasion, and are well-intentioned and loving the rest of the time. I would probably land on that list myself! Unfortunately, some individuals are intentionally or consistently malignant toward others as a way of being. It's important to identify who, or what, you're dealing with—again, with the help of a professional, if possible.

Here are my tips from that article, with some additional information I've found useful:

1. Minimize time spent interacting.
Keep your interactions as short as possible. Minimizing your exposure to difficult or upsetting individuals will minimize your own upset. It also gives them less of an opportunity to distort something that you've said, or use it to escalate an argument.

2. Keep it logical.
I'm a very verbal, heart-focused person, so I'd always try to connect with and reason with difficult people (and pretty much anyone else) from an emotional or empathic perspective. You know, those "when you do X it makes me feel Y" communication tactics from relationship books. This type of heart-centered communication only works with reasonable people who care. Difficult people often aren't interested in how you feel, and their response (or lack of it) to your vulnerable explanation may only make you more upset. Keep communications fact-based, using minimal details.

3. Don't drink in a difficult situation.
It's tempting to knock back a glass of wine or two when you're around someone who makes you feel stressed. Unfortunately, that can make you more emotionally vulnerable and more likely to do or say something that will make you look bad, feel bad, or make you more of a target.

4. Focus on them in conversation.
Again, a way to avoid being the target of upsetting comments, or having your words misinterpreted or dismissed, is to say as little as possible. If you have to spend time with or interact with a challenging individual, volunteer minimal information and get them talking about themselves. They're usually a safer conversation subject than you are.

5. Give up the dream that they'll become the person you wish they'd be.
There may be hurtful people in our lives who have moments where they seem to be the parent/partner/spouse/friend/colleague (insert whatever's appropriate) you've always felt they could be. You may let your guard down when you see this. Unfortunately, it often doesn't last, and they can end up hurting or disappointing you significantly. Yes, some people can truly change, but it takes a lot of work and is rare. Sometimes letting go of any hope for change, and fully accepting this person for who they really are, can be an unbelievable relief after a lifetime of wishing.

6. Stay away from topics that get you into trouble.
Before going into an interaction with a challenging individual, review in your mind the topics that invite attack or conflict and try to avoid them. For example, if your in-laws always make cracks about your choice of career, and they try to open the subject by asking you how work is going, answer neutrally and in as few words as possible. Next, change the subject immediately (see #4).

7. Don't try to get them to see your point of view.
This builds on what I shared in #2. If someone chronically treats you badly or mislabels you, don't spend a lot of time and energy trying to explain yourself. It's normal to want to help them understand you and empathize with your perspective. So many people make this mistake. It's natural to think that if someone could just understand you, they'd change their mind and treat you differently. It's fine to give this a try, or to make a short, firm statement in defense of yourself in important

contexts (for example, if it's in an important meeting). Generally, though, this type of person isn't interested in understanding you better, and you'll feel worse for trying.

8. Create a distraction.

If you have to spend time with someone who often upsets you or is hard on you, try to create circumstances that offer a distraction. Focus on playing with a pet if there's one in the vicinity. Base the interaction around some kind of recreational activity or entertainment, or offer to help in a way that takes you out of the line of fire. Offer to help out with something in the kitchen before a family dinner, as a way of getting out of the living room. If you can get them to do something that absorbs their attention (taking it off you), that's even better.

As you can see, boundary intelligence isn't just saying no to certain types of treatment and behaviors. Boundary-violating individuals often get upset, or even angry, if someone says no to them or calls them out on their behavior. Sometimes a clear no is what a situation requires, but you can also skillfully erect boundaries around yourself—for example, by sharing limited information or minimizing your participation in a conversation—without someone realizing that this is what you're doing.

These strategies are not about tolerating abuse. These techniques can be used to temporarily manage an abusive individual, but you always need to be aware of and evaluate your safety. My suggestions here do not replace the advice of a qualified counseling professional who understands your unique situation. If you are in a situation that is emotionally, verbally, or physically abusive, whether that be at home, at work, or in another context, please get help from whatever local resources are available to you. Your safety is your top priority, and abuse should never be tolerated or enabled.

BUILDING HEALTHY BOUNDARIES AT WORK

As a coach, I work with a variety of leaders (from mid-level managers to high-ranking executives, as well as entrepreneurs and business owners), helping them reduce their stress, recover from burnout, improve work-life balance, and operate more effectively.

Usually, after I do a little digging, a core problem emerges. Their lack of boundaries with coworkers or clients cause them to lose key time and energy, blocking them from optimal productivity and effectiveness. The constant interruptions and relentless bids for attention make workdays feel out of control. Stress gets maximized, and less "urgent" big-picture progress gets stalled.

A lack of boundaries causes you to take on workloads, priorities, or burdens that aren't yours to carry. The good news is that once you implement strategic boundaries and practices, your stress levels drop. You are more focused, are able to plan, and have more time and energy to get important things done. This improves your confidence and dials back concerns about your productivity and effectiveness, providing further protection against burnout.

Here are some tips that can help with core, common boundary challenges, helping you reduce unnecessary chaos and do your best work:

1. Set aside time to focus on your essential work.
First, identify what it is that you need to do that you're not getting done. Many leaders I coach complain that they get constant, excessive demands for attention. Pleas for help and unnecessary interruptions from their team or other people in the organization drive them to distraction. They struggle to devote time to critical high-level thinking or planning.

Figure out what you absolutely need to get done. If you're a leader, these are the core tasks and planning that only you can do. How many hours a week will you need to accomplish this? Decide when you could fit it into your schedule, and formally slot it in.

2. Protect that time for essential work.
There are different ways to do this. One client I worked with found that closing her door with a "Do Not Disturb" sign taped to it helped stop unnecessary interruptions. During that time, she logged off her email

and the office chat system. She informed her team that she would be regularly setting aside a certain time of day to work on key projects. No interruptions, except for emergencies.

Of course, she was tested. You will be, too. People will knock on the door. People will call. These instances usually aren't emergencies. Don't teach people that your words don't carry weight. Show them that when you set a boundary, you mean it. Be gracious, but make it clear that you need to do this. And tell them why. And empower them, too, to make some of these decisions on their own. That's good leadership.

In one case where people still wouldn't respect the request, my client started going somewhere else in the building to do their key work. Sometimes you have to do what you have to do. This isn't just for your own sanity and productivity; it's also for the benefit of the organization that hired you to do this work.

3. Stop taking on work that belongs to other people.
Again, I see this all the time. The leaders I work with are good at many things. Better than most other people, typically. They want everything to be done well—perfectly, even. As a result, they can't keep their hands off other people's tasks. Either they keep things on their plate that should really be done by others, or they hand off things but then micromanage or take over if they aren't being done exactly "right."

Does this sound familiar? To build truly healthy boundaries, you must create and enforce parameters around your own behavior. What do you need to stop doing? Ask yourself this, frequently.

If you really struggle to delegate, consider what tasks or items you have on your plate that are valuable opportunities for someone else to grow and develop. That perspective helps delegation feel more constructive and positive, if you're worried about burdening others.

4. Don't create (or reinforce) unrealistic, unnecessary expectations.
Are you the person who everyone counts on? That excess conscientiousness has a dark side. As I mentioned earlier, "extra-milers" are at high

risk for burnout, and for quitting their job altogether as a result of the pressures they put on themselves.

Take a moment to think about this: *Does your conscientiousness lead you to set standards for your work that others now expect from you that simply aren't necessary?*

In one case, a highly motivated account executive who served a prestigious list of clients had unwittingly "trained" them to expect him to respond to them immediately. To be available on weekends. To be available during vacations. It was probably part of his success, but it was also unsustainable. He was dangerously close to severe burnout, so something had to change.

As a start, he forced himself to take longer to respond to people. He'd offer to do for them what was appropriate, but not over the top. Next, he turned off his work phone and put it away, out of sight, on the weekends, not to be picked up until Monday morning. His clients and colleagues finally got an "out of office" auto-responder message when he went on vacation (and I did a happy dance).

The world didn't fall apart. In fact, when he did this in conjunction with other positive changes, such as drinking less alcohol to cope, getting enough sleep, taking Sundays fully off, and doing relaxation practices, he felt like a new person in a matter of months. He started to enjoy his work more again, too.

If these steps feel out of reach for you in your situation, I encourage you to smart small. Look for any opportunity to improve your boundaries and decrease unnecessary, unreasonable expectations in your work environment. You will find them if you start looking! I would bet that there are a number of things that you can control and improve, simply by becoming aware of them and implementing new, firm changes. Changes that help you do your best work, with much less stress.

COACHING EXERCISE

I encourage you to closely examine the things in your work life that frustrate you and cause you stress.

What are you doing, or agreeing to do, that isn't really necessary and makes your day exhausting?

Where and how can you adjust your actions to realign people's expectations?

How can you set your day (and your boundaries) up so that your true priorities get done?

Talk to your colleagues and clients about any changes you plan to make, to assist them in readjusting their expectations.

INCREASE YOUR CONTROL OF KEY WORK-LIFE BOUNDARIES

One of my favorite investigations of the impact of work-life balance was done by Dr. Leslie Perlow, PhD, and Jessica Porter at Harvard Business School. They demonstrated in the notoriously intense environment of the Boston Consulting Group (BCG) that "it is perfectly possible for consultants and other professionals to meet the highest standards of service and still have planned, uninterrupted time off."[1]

One of their experimental interventions was to require each consultant to take one scheduled night off per week. After six o'clock, the consultant couldn't do any work, including checking or responding to emails or any other type of message. One project manager's response, which is very typical, was this: "What good is a night off going to do? Won't it force me to work more on weekends?"

As it turned out, the participants in this experiment reported higher job satisfaction, more open communication, increased learning and development, and a better product delivered to the client. Sure, they were just taking one night off a week, but the takeaway is that protected time off from work, within your day-to-day personal life, will likely have significant positive impacts on both yourself and your work.

Maybe six o'clock can't be your cut-off every night, but choose something that works for you. Try to formally create a work-free night in your schedule as often as you can. Having clear boundaries around where your work stops and your non-work life begins is one of the best things you can do for both your own well-being and your success on the job.

As a result of the pandemic, a huge number of people pivoted to working from home, at least part of the time. This shift, which naturally blurs the lines between one's work and home life, has made work-life boundaries more important than ever. Dr. Ellen Kossek, PhD, one of the leading researchers and experts in this area, details differing boundary management styles and helpful strategies in a 2016 article on "Managing work-life boundaries in the digital age."[2]

According to Kossek, "effectively managing work-life boundaries can not only reduce work-life conflicts, but can also reduce stress, burnout, addictions, mood disorders and enhance mental and physical health." If you're a leader, enhancing your competence in this area can also help you be more effective in your management and support of others. Kossek emphasizes key self-management strategies that can help increase your "personal boundary control." Here are my favorites, including some of my thoughts on each:

1. Manage the transitions.
In our nonstop, "always-on" working world, we can easily bring our work self and work-related thoughts and emotions into our personal life. For example, you might go straight from an intense, stressful meeting into dinner with your family. If possible, give yourself time to transition. Kossek suggests that when you're driving home from work, you can intentionally avoid thinking about work problems and get yourself into a zone where you're ready to socialize with your family when you get home. Listen to music you enjoy, or a non-work-related podcast or audiobook.

If you're working from home and can't use a commute to decompress, find other ways to create these transitions (in this context, this may be even more important, as it's so easy to carry work into your personal life when you don't ever leave the "office"). I often go for a walk with my dog after I finish my day, or I might curl up on the couch to read the news before even thinking about dinner.

2. Create time buffers.
Despite the temptation to squeeze the most out of your schedule, try to avoid booking things back-to-back. If you pack your calendar too tightly, you'll inevitably run long and be late sometimes, making your day feel more stressful whenever it happens. No one needs more stress! Also, whenever you have to prep for a meeting or drive to an appointment, give yourself more time than you need. Do whatever you can to minimize the amount of running late, pushing, or rushing in your life. Just five extra minutes can make all the difference.

3. Separate your devices, if possible.
Use different devices (phones, laptops, tablets, etc.) for work and home, if you can. Tuck your work phone away when you don't need it. One of my clients would put hers in a designated drawer when she got home, so she wouldn't be tempted to pick it up randomly. And do your best to keep your work phone, or your work, out of your bedroom. Don't check email in bed, ever. Get an alarm clock, if you insist that that's why you need to keep that phone on your bedside table. Yes, I've heard that excuse too many times!

It's also important to prevent unnecessary interruptions from breaking your workflow. Every time something distracts you from what you're doing, you experience "process losses." You then waste time and energy to get back into the zone of what you were doing. I like to put my personal phone on "do not disturb" mode when working. That way, nothing pings at me and distracts me. I can check to see if I've received any messages when I take a break. You can typically program these modes so that important calls or texts from certain contacts, like your spouse or your child's daycare center, will still come through.

5. Manage your space boundaries at home.
Build as many physical boundaries between your work and personal life as possible, when working from home. Close the door to your home office, if you have one, and don't go back in during non-work times, if you can avoid it. If you don't have a dedicated office, avoid leaving your work laptop or work-related papers out when switching into family or personal time. Turn your work phone off and put it away. Make it a habit to put everything work-related away when you make the switch. Your home and your free time will feel much lighter. Try to build a clear "work is done" moment into your day, rather than constantly flowing back and forth between your life and work.

6. Strive to be mentally present (whatever you're doing).
Again, it's important to cultivate the discipline of being present with whatever you're engaged in, whether it's work or play. Similar to what I recommended in my discussion of the value of mindfulness, Kossek suggests that one should "strive for mindfulness to be physically present in the moment wherever you are working … during personal time, psychologically detach from work to focus on family and personal life." She also recommends, as I do, that you organize specific blocks of time to focus exclusively on key tasks or projects.

7. Set aside time to focus on yourself.
If you're trying to work from home, you may feel constantly torn between work and family demands, or social demands if you have room-mates. These two competing interests can split you so intensely that you forget that you need time for yourself, too. Find ways to schedule breaks for yourself in your day that are just for you. Plan in some exercise, or take time to enjoy your lunch. I sometimes hide in my office with a sandwich and watch part of a movie on my laptop. Sometimes you need to recharge on your own. It's OK. And it can be necessary.

COACHING EXERCISE

Reflect on the ways that work can invade your personal life.

1.   What are five ways that your work tends to negatively impact your personal life? (e.g., after-hours emails or calls, thinking about it when you're with your family, reminders of your work in your personal space)

2.   Using these five ways, come up with five strategies to improve those boundaries (e.g., no checking email after six o'clock).

PART V

BUILD A FOUNDATION OF PHYSICAL RESILIENCE

9

HOW TO SLEEP BETTER

In my experience, books and teachings on how to increase resilience tend to mention physical resilience as a side note, if it's mentioned at all. I can't imagine leaving this out. The strategies that I share in the next three chapters have been absolute game-changers for me. I can't emphasize enough what a difference they make to my ability to cope with life and rise above stress and challenges. I've seen their impact again and again, in patients and coaching clients, too. Enhanced physical well-being reliably increases your ability to navigate stress, change, pressure, and life in general.

And yes, I'm aware that it's not news to anyone that sleep, optimal nutrition, and exercise can enhance all aspects of your well-being and performance. My hope is that some of the fresh, evidence-based facts that I share, along with strategies and techniques that can really help shift your behavior, will give you the insights, motivation, and skills to lock in excellent habits in these areas.

Let's say that, like many people in our society, you haven't had a good night's sleep in ages. Most people need seven to eight hours of sleep a night. Sadly, you typically get around six hours. As a result, you're more irritable, moody, and anxious. You struggle to solve problems, make decisions, and manage stress. You might be so used to feeling this way that you believe you're just a chronically anxious, stressed-out person.

In an article published in *Nature* in 2019, UC Berkeley's Dr. Eti Ben Simon, PhD, and colleagues noted that sleep provides a significant "overnight anxiety-reduction benefit." Lack of sleep amplifies feelings of anxiety in a direct dose-response matter. And "even modest night-to-night reductions in sleep across the population predict consequential day-to-day increases in anxiety."[1]

For a lot of us, sleep is the magic game-changing pill we've been waiting and wishing for. Speaking of pills, "sleeping pills" don't really work that well. They can be helpful if you're going through a short-term crisis and need something to help you sleep for a few days. They're not meant for long-term use, though. Most sleep medications can cause dependency, along with nasty long-lasting side effects in critical areas such as memory and cognitive function. The lasting solution for most sleep problems is understanding how sleep biology works and what habits best support it (with the help of an expert, if necessary).

You may be well aware of how sleep deprived you are. You feel like garbage. You know you should get more sleep. It's just too hard to find time for; there aren't enough hours in the day. Or you've tried to go to bed earlier, but you can't fall asleep when you do. Maybe you've been waking up in the middle of the night and struggle to get back to sleep, or you wake up too early in the morning. So, what are you supposed to do? In this chapter, we'll get into all of this and more. Even if you sleep well and enough most of the time, there are tips and strategies here that can supercharge this most essential restorative health practice.

LET'S START BY INCREASING YOUR MOTIVATION TO SLEEP

Often, you know you should make a change in your life, but you can't get yourself to shift from knowing it to *doing* it. It really frustrates you. What's wrong with you? Well, you're human. Humans find it hard to make changes that require new behaviors, if they don't have a big enough "why."

Whenever bedtime approaches, other things can seem more important. Like having more time to relax in the evening. Or getting those last few late-night emails in to keep your manager happy. I get it. I've been there.

Here are some "why's" that can help you feel more motivated to prioritize sleep:

1. Your mental health depends on it.

Not all mental health problems can be solved by sleep, but if you're not sleeping well, it pummels your mental health.

Many psychological and psychiatric disorders have disturbed sleep as a common symptom. It's only more recently, though, that researchers have been focusing on the fact that sleep problems may actually lead to mental health problems, rather than just being a symptom of poor mental health. I've observed this pattern in myself, and in patients and clients, for a long time.

Another paper published by UC Berkeley's Dr. Allison Harvey, PhD, and colleagues (she was a coauthor on the paper in *Nature*) reported that "sleep disturbance is increasingly recognized as an important, but under-studied, mechanism in the complex and multi-factorial causation of the symptoms and functional disability associated with psychiatric disorders."[2]

Experiment to find out how much sleep you need, and observe the impact on your mood. When I work with executives and leaders, many claim they don't need much sleep to function at their best. This may (rarely) be true, but I often challenge them to run an experiment. You can try this, too: If you normally sleep just six hours, try getting seven hours and see if you feel any different. Then try getting eight hours. Do you notice an impact on your mood and energy levels? Most people do. (And of course, if no matter what you do, you can't seem to improve your sleep, please talk to your doctor.)

If I get eight hours or more a night, I feel amazing. If I get seven hours, I feel OK, but not fabulous. If I get less than seven hours, I start to feel fried and irritable. Know what your "magic sleep number" is for you. Play around with it until you know where you're at your best. Then aim for it every night. Why would you not want to feel great and be at your best? (And if it's not that simple for you—for example, perhaps you suffer from insomnia—we'll talk about that.)

2. Sleep could give you the edge you need to get that promotion.
"Sleep Inspires Insight," according to another article published in *Nature* by Dr. Ullrich Wagner, PhD, and colleagues.[3] This research was inspired by accounts of famous scientific discoveries that were related to or triggered by sleep. Mendeleyev, for example, discovered the critical rule underlying the periodic table of elements after having a dream.

In this *Nature* study, test subjects were trained in certain sequences. Apparently, there was a "hidden abstract rule" that would enable them to suddenly improve their performance, which twice as many subjects discovered after they got eight hours of nighttime sleep. The conclusion: sleep restructures our memories in a way that enables fresh insight.

According to a 2019 clinical review called "Why Healthy Sleep is Good for Business,"[4] well-rested employees miss less work,[5] do a better job,[5] make better decisions,[6] and interact more positively with others.[7]

One of my favorite speeches of all time was given by leadership expert Michael Hyatt, at Leadercast 2018.[8] He powerfully characterized self-care as an essential discipline for leaders. The bigger your vision, he emphasized, the more you need to prioritize self-care. Sleeping enough is at the top of his list of key daily habits. Hyatt referenced neuroscientists who had demonstrated that sleep-deprived people come up with fewer original ideas and tend to stick with old strategies. "An extra hour of sleep," he said, "might be your best strategy for innovation."

3. If you want to lose (or stop gaining) weight, sleep may help you move that needle.

At another lecture I attended at Harvard's Institute for Lifestyle Medicine, I listened to Dr. Lee Kaplan, MD, PhD, of the Obesity, Metabolism and Nutrition Institute at Massachusetts General Hospital speak on "Obesity and Metabolic Risk."[9] He mentioned sleep multiple times, including the fact that people gain weight when sleep deprived. Sleep deprivation and altered circadian rhythms, he pointed out, can be key environmental drivers of obesity via their direct impact on certain brain areas, playing a role in raising one's fat mass set point. "Sleep enhancement" was on his list of current and emerging treatments of obesity related to lifestyle.

In accordance with the information that Kaplan shared, the Harvard T.H. Chan School of Public Health reports that several studies show that sleep deprivation (regularly getting less than seven hours of sleep a night) is a risk factor for obesity.[10] We've known for quite a while now that lack of sleep disrupts hormones that regulate our appetite. Ghrelin, a hunger hormone that increases when you're sleep deprived, stimulates your appetite and makes you more likely to eat high-fat, high-carb foods. How unfair is that?

Poor sleep can also increase belly fat, lead to a poorer quality diet, and decrease insulin sensitivity, a key driver of your metabolism.[11,12] You'll also feel less like exercising.

Though obesity and weight loss are complex, multifaceted challenges, we know enough about the links between sleep, metabolism, and weight to strongly recommend that you cultivate good sleep habits if you wish to reach or stay at a healthy weight. After all, the side effects of this "intervention" are pretty amazing. You'll feel better, cope better, have more energy, and you'll probably even look younger, too.

KEY HABITS AND STRATEGIES FOR BETTER SLEEP

Alex, the CEO of a large non-profit, was exhausted. I asked about sleep, as I always do.

"I'm a really light sleeper," he told me. "I wake up all the time. It feels like I'm up most of the night, and I feel like a zombie most days."

I asked about caffeine. He used to drink too much coffee, but had replaced it with carbonated water a while ago. So, what was wrecking his sleep? Perhaps he had a sleep disorder or was under too much stress?

Neither, it turned out. I asked more questions and discovered that Alex, like too many others, went to bed with his phone. He worried he'd miss an important or urgent message, so he kept notifications on. His phone buzzed all night long. If he had to go to the bathroom during the night, he'd bring his phone and check email. He'd usually see a message or messages that got his mind going, and he wouldn't be able to fall back asleep.

Alex was a "sleep hygiene" disaster! Thankfully, these issues were easy to fix. First, we silenced his notifications. Most phones have options for controlling notifications to facilitate sleep or productivity (I put my phone into "airplane mode" along with "do not disturb" mode before I go to bed). He also committed to stop checking email in the middle of the night. Perhaps most importantly, he came up with a system that would give him more backup coverage from others. He stopped being the go-to person for midnight emergencies.

Within days of our first conversation, he was sleeping undisturbed, all night long. And he found fresh energy to face his days. You may not relate to his experience (I haven't met anyone else who lets their phone ping all night long). Still, I've found that the things that I'm going to discuss here apply to the lives and habits of many people. I should also note that I'm only getting into solutions for the most common, relatively benign sleep challenges. Again, if you're really struggling with sleep, please see your doctor.

Here are some of the top strategies that have helped me, my patients, and my clients to sleep better:

1. Intentionally wind down at night.

I often start here, with busy, stressed people who are having trouble falling asleep and staying asleep. If you're in that category, there's a strong probability that you're overstimulating yourself and your brain in the evenings. So many of my coaching clients take work home, or work from home, and have the habit of checking email and doing other tasks at night. You may even feel like that's the best time, as the kids are in bed and the house is quiet.

If you feel tired all the time, are exhausted by the end of your day, but can't turn your mind off when you go to bed, get serious about winding down. Choose a time after which you won't check email or do anything work-related. Ideally, make this the time after which you also won't look at any screen. This strategy also helps with burnout prevention, better job satisfaction, and increased productivity, as demonstrated by the research from Perlow and Porter.[13]

Beyond removing work stress, minimize or eliminate other activities that stress you out or wake you up in the evening. Reduce your caffeine intake, too. If you've been having trouble falling asleep, avoid having coffee or tea beyond your first cup in the morning, and consider eliminating it entirely. Be conscious of other sources of caffeine, as well, such as energy drinks, kombucha, carbonated drinks, and chocolate. I'm very sensitive to caffeine and have observed that snacking on chocolate in the evening can make it hard for me to fall asleep.

Don't exercise before bedtime, and avoid difficult conversations. I have a rule that I don't start any difficult conversations after eight o'clock, because my fretful mind won't be able to fall asleep afterward. Also, I've heard several sleep experts caution against texting or messaging at or near bedtime, as these interactions wake up your brain more than passive reading. Avoid scrolling through your social feed before or at bedtime, as you may see something that upsets you. Same goes for reading the news, or watching it in bed. I know people who like to watch the news right before turning off the light. A bright, blue-light-emanating television screen that spews out negative news at bedtime equals one of the worst ideas imaginable.

> **COACHING EXERCISE**
>
> *Reflect on what you normally do in the evenings.*
>
> *Are there activities that you regularly do that are stimulating?*
>
> *How could you eliminate them, or move them to an earlier time?*
>
> *What are some things that you could do to make your evenings feel more relaxing, to help your brain and body wind down and prepare for a good night's sleep?*

2. If poor sleep is a problem, keep a sleep log for a few days.
At the same Lifestyle Medicine course, I heard Dr. Eric Zhou, PhD, from Harvard Medical School's Division of Sleep Medicine, lecture on the most effective lifestyle interventions for "Sleep Problems."[14] He referred to the primary criterion for the diagnosis of insomnia: being dissatisfied with the quantity or quality of your sleep for three or more nights a week, for more than three months.[15] Shocked, I realized that that applied to me!

In line with the clinical practice guideline of the American College of Physicians,[16] Zhou emphasized that the first-line treatment for insomnia is CBT-I, or cognitive behavioral therapy for insomnia. The core components of this approach include: sleep restriction; stimulus control (e.g., avoiding using your bed for things other than intimacy and sleep); sleep hygiene; cognitive challenges; and relaxation exercises. I've heard other sleep researchers call CBT-I the most effective treatment for the vast majority of cases of insomnia. You can learn more about CBT-I from popular books on the subject, as well as through apps and, ideally, with help from a specially trained doctor, psychologist, or counselor.

The first step is to observe what's actually happening, by keeping a sleep log. You'll find lots of sample logs online. There are also various sleep-tracking apps. A smartwatch can be useful, too, though it may not be entirely accurate at tracking sleep. That said, these days I use an Apple Watch to capture basic sleep data, and use an app called SleepWatch to record and track the information.

After arriving home from Boston, I made up my own log in the back of my journal. For two weeks, I kept track of the following:

- The time I started getting ready for bed (if it was unusually late, I noted why)

- The time I turned the lights out

- The approximate time that I fell asleep (approximate, because you should avoid checking the time after you've gone to bed)

- The approximate amount of time it took to fall asleep

- The time I woke up

- The number of hours I was actually asleep

- The number of total hours in bed (this is used to calculate "sleep efficiency")

- Whether I had had wine the day prior

- Whether I had exercised the day prior

- General quality of sleep

- How I felt the next day

For seven of fourteen nights, I slept less than seven hours—some nights, six hours or less. *What?* My sleep had gotten this bad without my realizing how bad it was.

When I looked at the log, on the worst nights I started getting ready for bed after eleven o'clock. It was usually because we'd stayed out late or stayed up late chatting. On several occasions, we arrived home from road trips much later than planned. My wake-up time was also erratic, and undesirably early, after those late nights.

I made a plan. I'd start getting ready for bed shortly after ten o'clock every night, as those were the nights I had gotten my best rest. Lights out before eleven. If we were out, or driving in from somewhere, we had to try to leave on time to be home by ten at the latest.

I aimed to get up at seven o'clock, to maintain a consistent wake-up time (more on that in the sleep tips that follow). As soon as I woke, I'd go into the living room and open the blinds to expose myself to daylight (more on that in a moment, too). After just one week, the impact was remarkable. I'd expected to have to implement the "sleep restriction" process, the next step in CBT-I, where you calculate the number of hours you actually sleep per night, and then set strict bedtime hours where you're not allowed to physically be in bed for more than that amount of time. Instead, I continued to keep a log, and within a couple of weeks, I was sleeping seven to eight hours a night, every single night. And I was sleeping much more soundly. It was like a miracle.

COACHING EXERCISE

Try keeping a sleep log, using the list above.

You'll find a sample sleep log in the workbook, or you could track this information in a journal or on a notes app on your phone. You don't have to track all the things that I did, just what seems helpful to you. There are also many apps out there that track sleep data for you.

After a week or two of tracking, is there any information or pattern that jumps out at you?

Does anything surprise you?

What does it tell you about where you could improve, or what you could do differently and more intentionally, when it comes to your sleep?

Adjust your habits based on what you observe.

(Note: It really just takes a few seconds to make your notes after you wake up, but if it feels like too much for you to do right now, I've got some other easy-to-implement recommendations.)

3. Prime your brain for sleep by using a light strategy.

Your exposure to light, both natural and artificial, at different points in your day, determines both your levels of daytime alertness (when you want and need to be awake and focused) and your ability to fall asleep at night.

I must offer an important caveat, however: in my experience and based on my own review of related literature, an early morning light strategy is very helpful for (most) people who have difficulty falling asleep or have trouble getting up in the morning. If you get sleepy early in the evening and fall asleep easily, but find yourself waking much earlier than you want to, you may have a different kind of circadian rhythm issue in which your sleep cycle has advanced too far in reverse. In this case, early morning light may exacerbate your situation, winding back your circadian clock to wake up even earlier. You might need brighter lighting in the evening, to help your body stay awake longer so you can sleep in later. It can be tricky. As always, if you're experiencing significant challenges, consult an expert.

That said, it's usually helpful to expose yourself to natural light first thing in the morning, shortly after waking up. Try to get outside first thing, for whatever amount of time you can manage. A few minutes will do, but longer is better. Enhance the impact with some exercise, if you can; a morning walk or run works well.

This gets your mind and body going for your day, and also primes your brain to produce melatonin, the sleep hormone in the evening, when you'll want to go to sleep. Make these activities part of your daily rhythm.

Your body loves consistent routines and patterns. Going to sleep and waking up at the same time, followed by early morning light exposure and exercise, trains your body to sleep more easily and efficiently.

Next, avoid bright lights in the evening (of all kinds, not just screens; I'll say more about devices in a moment). After the sun goes down, keep your lights down. Avoid brightly lit restaurants, stores, or other environments. Bright artificial light in the evening inhibits melatonin release and increases your alertness. In the evening, you want your brain to wind down and prepare for sleep.

Again, if you're someone who falls asleep early and easily, and wakes too early, you may need to follow a different practice. If you're not sure which would be most helpful to you, consider trying both approaches to evening light and see which one improves your sleep the most.

Regardless of your circadian tendency, avoid exposing yourself to bright light if you have to get up in the night. Keep the lights as low as you safely can, or have soft night-lights on in hallways or bathrooms. Avoid having a night-light in your bedroom, as the darker it is, the better you'll sleep.

Now, about your screens and that dreaded blue light. If you've been having trouble sleeping, take this very seriously. When I get sloppy and indulge in late-night phone scrolling or reading, I always end up frustrated by how hard it is to fall and stay asleep.

I frequently tell audiences about a favorite study from the Division of Sleep Medicine at Harvard, where they compared the impact of using an e-reader versus reading a good old-fashioned printed book, for four hours before bedtime.[17] Those who read the e-book took longer to fall asleep, delayed their circadian clocks (bad if you want to go to bed at a decent time and get a full night's rest), had suppressed melatonin levels, experienced delayed and reduced REM sleep, and were less alert the following morning. I've seen lives changed and insomnia "cured" when clients have taken the simple step of switching to a real-book reading habit before bed. A paper book is such an enjoyable escape from our always-on tech world, too.

If you absolutely must use a device in the evening—let's face it, most of us are addicted—turn the screen brightness down as far as you can, and set up any apps or features that shift the screen colors after sunset. An iPhone, for example, comes with a "night shift" option. Use glasses that block blue light. A caution: Don't use these glasses round the clock, as during the day, you want blue light to increase alertness and signal to your brain that it's daytime, not bedtime.

COACHING EXERCISE

If you've been struggling with insomnia, see what happens if, for a night, you avoid all screens and read a "real" book instead.

This exercise doesn't have a written component—I just want you to try this!

I predict that you'll find yourself getting deliciously sleepy, and fall asleep—and stay asleep—more easily than usual. If you notice a difference, consider making this a new habit.

4. Keep your bedtime and wake time as consistent as you can.
This was part of the strategy I implemented after hearing that sleep lecture in Boston. As my sleep had improved, however, I'd gotten more careless about my sleep schedule again. This wasn't a problem for several years, until I experienced a number of stressful events over the last few months. I developed the most severe insomnia I've ever experienced.

Some nights, especially if something stressful had happened in the evening, I had trouble falling asleep. Other times, I woke up in the middle of the night and it took hours to fall back asleep. I also frequently woke up a couple of hours earlier than I wanted to, and that was it for the night. It was awful.

First, I should mention that I started by targeting the stress. My body was telling me that something was wrong; the insomnia was really just a symptom. My profoundly disturbed sleep forced me to take a closer look at my life. I started seeing a counselor to process the stressful situations, met with my doctor to let her know what was happening, incorporated healthier boundaries into my life, made sure I was spending time with (and leaning on) friends, increased my exercise, used breathing throughout the day to calm my nervous system, and made sure I was doing at least ten minutes of mindfulness daily.

I also started keeping a sleep log again, and reviewed some of the key principles of CBT-I (such as getting out of bed any time you're lying awake at night, and going somewhere else in your home until you feel sleepy again). I also knew that I had to get my circadian clock back on track. The best way to do this? Strictly regimented sleep and wake-up times.

Based on my sleep log, my most common sleep time was now 9:45 p.m. I'd been going to bed earlier and earlier, to compensate for waking up early. Not the smartest thing to do, by the way. I wanted to reset my sleep clock to get a full eight hours, so I started setting an alarm for 6:00 a.m. It was tempting to let myself sleep in (if that miracle occurred), but I knew that the best thing for my body would be strict routine.

I'd also gotten into the (terrible, anxiety-provoking, and sleep-stealing) habit of checking the time whenever I woke up in the night. In addition to eliminating the risk of oversleeping, setting an alarm helped me tell myself that there was no reason to check the time, if or when I woke up in the dark.

So, I got to bed by 9:45 p.m. every night, even if it meant curtailing evening activities. If I woke up in the night for what felt like more than twenty minutes, I would get out of bed and do something quiet and relaxing until I felt sleepy again. Interestingly, once I committed to my new strict sleep/wake schedule, the mid-night awakenings became much shorter and I hardly had to practice this response.

As with my previous post-Boston story, this sleep routine strategy worked so well that I didn't have to move to the sleep-restriction step of CBT-I. Within a week, I got a full night's sleep seven days in a row.

I could hardly believe it, as it had been months since I had slept that well. I stopped waking in the night altogether and also started waking up naturally, minutes before the alarm went off.

Sleep is truly a biologically-driven phenomenon. When you honor and follow the fundamental principles and schedule that your body prefers for sleep, the results can be amazing.

10

MAKE FOOD WORK FOR YOU, NOT AGAINST YOU

I've been passionate about nutrition since I was a teenager, and I obtained a degree in dietetics before entering medical school. I also wrote a monthly national nutrition column for Canada's doctors and health care professionals for eight years. This chapter isn't just about eating for a healthy, more resilient brain—it's about fueling a high-performing brain. If you make strategic food choices, you'll be better equipped to handle challenging problems at work. You'll be more likely to excel in situations that require a good memory, rapid mental processing, or a quick response.

If you're someone who struggles with doing things just because they're "healthy," think about nutrition in terms of your performance and your long-term success. As we get older, our cognitive function naturally declines, becoming noticeable for many of us as we move through our forties. Ageism is bad enough in this world. One way to fight back, and keep your edge, is by giving your brain the very best fuel possible.

HOW TO KNOW WHAT TO EAT

I know, it's so hard to navigate all the information. How can you know what's true, when studies support both sides of every nutritional controversy? Won't the "right" answers just change next year, anyway?

I've been following information and trends in nutrition for over thirty years. I'm wary of fads, any popular way of eating based on extreme food choices or behaviors, and anything that promises magical or fast results. Across the years, though, below all the noise, certain fundamentals have stood the test of time. Backed by ongoing scientific evidence, these also represent a reasonable, sustainable approach to eating.

For any healthy eating practices or choices to stick, they have to be reasonably enjoyable (and ideally, very enjoyable). They also have to fit into your lifestyle over the long haul. Ideally, nourishing yourself wisely and well becomes a way of life. You keep doing it because it works, it's relatively easy, you feel great, and you now enjoy eating this way. That's how I feel about the way I eat. It's not a struggle. It's a source of joy, well-being, and life.

A word about trendy diets and nutrition fads: If you've found a popular way of eating that really works for you, I'm not suggesting you change it (this isn't, and never will be, medical advice; it's just information). For example, if the keto diet is your thing, and it has helped you lose weight and keep it off, and you have way more energy, I'm not here to argue with you. I trust that you're talking to your doctor about what you're doing, getting appropriate blood tests and monitoring, that you know the risks and drawbacks and so on. You might find, though, that you end up changing some of your protein or vegetable sources or patterns, after reading the information here.

Also, what works best for you may not work for someone else, and vice versa. We're learning how genetic and other differences lead to different outcomes for different people. A study published in *Diabetes Care* in 2016 looked at the relationship between a certain genotype (FGF21) and the success of different types of weight-loss diets.[1] They found that people who possessed a certain genetic marker, the "C allele," lost the most body fat, inches from their waist, and trunk fat when on a low-calorie, high-carb, low-fat diet (a very untrendy way of eating). This group had the opposite outcome with a high-fat/low-carb diet. So, as popular as it might be, a low-carb diet wouldn't be the right path to weight loss for someone with this genetic background. It's complicated. Still, I believe that the fundamentals I'm about to focus on will be useful and relevant to most people. They're also not for the purpose of weight loss, though the choices I discuss may take pounds off as a side effect.

CHOOSE FOODS THAT BOOST YOUR BRAIN AND YOUR MOOD
Because of my history of depression during my residency training, I became interested in the power of food to support my brain and promote a positive mood.

Let's talk about food and mental health, a.k.a. "nutritional psychiatry." It's well established that our food choices impact our brains and our moods. Certain foods give life to our brain, while others inflame and irritate it, and make it more sluggish.

The dietary pattern most strongly associated with decreased rates of depression is what's known as the Mediterranean diet. People who eat this way consume lots of fish, olive oil, vegetables, fruits, legumes, nuts, and fiber-rich whole grains. They also eat less red meat and saturated fats. The Mediterranean diet's original claim to fame came from its cardiovascular and metabolic health benefits, but it's also good for your brain and mental health.

In 2019, a team led by researchers from the Department of Epidemiology and Public Health at University College London published a review paper on the link between healthy dietary factors and risk of depressive outcomes.[2] They reported that "adhering to a healthy diet, in particular a traditional Mediterranean diet, or avoiding a pro-inflammatory diet appears to confer some protection against depression in observational studies." They noted that there is sufficient evidence to assess the role of dietary interventions to prevent depression. I love reports like this, and there's lots of other research that supports this position.

THE LINK BETWEEN FOOD AND INFLAMMATION

The University College London researchers recommended avoiding a "pro-inflammatory diet." I've talked about the risks of inflammation for a long time. As you'll see, this concept is important not only for your mental resilience but also for your long-term physical health and well-being.

Years ago, after moving to Mexico, I experienced yet another bout of frustrating acne. To give you some background, I'd been on the powerful anti-acne drug Accutane a couple of times already. The first time was for chronic cystic acne during medical school. My dermatologist said the severe acne was caused by stress combined with hormones, and put me on the medication. The second time my skin flared badly was a few years later, after a trip to Italy. I'll never forget my first post-Italy day at the medical clinic. A colleague actually asked me: "What happened to your face?" (Please don't ever say that to someone with acne. It's not very nice.) Other than that comment, there wasn't any stress involved this time. Just lots of gelato, crusty bread, and creamy pastas. I saw another dermatologist, and more Accutane was prescribed.

My skin cleared up for a few years again, until the move to Mexico. At the time, I was primarily focused on writing and flamenco dancing, but would fly back north periodically to work as a doctor. On one of my trips back home, I saw a dermatologist that a colleague had recommended.

"Are you eating a lot of corn?" he asked me. Yes. I'd even learned how to make tortillas from scratch and was pretty proud of it. I was also eating lots of sugary yogurts, and other foods that convert quickly to sugar in the bloodstream. He told me that these high-glycemic foods

(foods that elevate blood sugar levels) were causing inflammation. This was probably the main reason that my acne had flared.

In 2014, researchers from the University of South Carolina updated the Dietary Inflammatory Index, a tool that categorizes individuals' diets on a continuum from maximally anti-inflammatory to maximally pro-inflammatory.[3] Scores are based on a variety of very specific food parameters. Cholesterol and saturated fat (representative of animal meats, especially red meat), carbohydrates, and trans fats (found in processed foods) are considered markers of a pro-inflammatory diet. In contrast, omega-3 fatty acids (found in fish), and vitamins, antioxidant flavonoids, and carotenoids (prevalent in fruits and vegetables) are examples of anti-inflammatory food components. Other notable anti-inflammatory food parameters listed include turmeric, green or black tea, and ginger.

This isn't just about having clear skin. Inflamed skin points to more widespread inflammation in the body. A 2021 review article in *Advances in Nutrition* studied the connection between measures of Dietary Inflammatory Index (DII) and chronic disease risk.[4] They reported convincing evidence between a pro-inflammatory diet and heart attacks, and highly suggestive evidence linking these dietary patterns with increased all-cause mortality and risk of colorectal, pancreatic, respiratory, and oral cancers.

The dermatologist gave me a list of foods to avoid, recommended some resources to read, and sent me on my way. No Accutane this time, just some recommendations for topical treatments that normally had never helped.

I immediately changed what I was eating, and my face cleared up quickly. And I was amazed by what I read in those resources he had recommended, about the link between certain foods and inflammation in the body. I also learned that blood sugar spikes from high-glycemic foods could cross-link collagen and accelerate wrinkle formation and skin aging. From that point on, I was on a mission to save anyone I could from food-provoked inflammation. And I admit, I was pretty fired up about eating in a way that would slow down skin aging. I still am!

A GUIDE TO FOODS FOR BRAIN HEALTH

What happens when you take a group of otherwise healthy, sedentary, overweight men and women with high blood pressure, and have them eat a diet rich in vegetables, fruits, whole grains, fish, poultry, beans, and nuts for four months? Their brain function improves.

Participants in this 2010 study, published in *Hypertension*, who changed the way they ate improved their psychomotor speed.[5] They responded more quickly to changes in their environment. Those who added exercise and reduced caloric intake on top of the nutritional changes experienced improvements in executive function and memory learning, as well as increased psychomotor speed. According to neuroscience experts, this was the equivalent of performing as if they were nine years younger, on tests of reading and writing speed.[6] Incredible.

Based on this and other research, a group of Canadian scientists and experts in nutrition and neuroscience created the *Brain Health Food Guide*.[6] I love this easy-to-understand, easy-to-follow guide to the best foods for your brain. It's not a diet. It's about smart food choices, and brilliantly illustrates the type of balance you should aim for. The *Guide* lists optimal daily and weekly frequencies for each type of food, so you can use it to guide your meal planning, if that's your thing.

I encourage you to have a look at the *Guide* for specific serving amounts (you'll find the link in the References section), but I'll give you the basics:

- Eat lots of vegetables, including raw leafy greens, once a day.

- Eat lots of fruit, especially berries (your brain loves all those bright antioxidant compounds).

- Eat unsalted nuts or nut butter every day, with walnuts several times a week. (Not only do walnuts look like little brains, they contain polyphenols that reduce brain cell inflammation and increase neural signaling and new neuron formation in the brain.[7])

- Have beans or legumes at least a couple of times a week. (You don't have to cook these from scratch; I stock our kitchen with high-quality soups and packaged stews made from whole food ingredients that can be ready in minutes on the stovetop.)

- Fish or seafood is recommended three times a week.

- Olive oil is suggested as your main culinary oil for cooking and dressings.

- Eat whole grains instead of "white," refined carbohydrate sources.

Foods to limit, which negatively impact your brain, include meat and poultry, which are limited to no more than one meal a day, with red and processed meats being limited to less than one serving per week. Baked goods, dairy desserts, candy, and so on should also be consumed in minimal amounts. I really appreciate that they don't say that you can't eat these things—which many people would find really hard to do—but instead illustrate where and how these foods fit in, if you want to limit their negative impact on your cognitive capacity and brain function.

BREAK THE HABIT OF STRESS-EATING AND EMOTIONAL EATING

"Sure," you might say to me, "this is all great. I know I should eat healthy foods, but I blow it all the time. I'm stressed out and too busy. I grab what's fastest, what tastes best, and what makes me feel better in the moment. And that's not a vegetable."

The struggle is real.

Erica, an executive who I've coached for a long time, is one of the most determined, focused people I know. She also highly values health. When she's in a good zone (read: less stress, fewer project deadlines and less fires to put out at work), she loves to go for runs, goes to Pilates several times a week, and loves making beautiful, nutritious meals.

When things get tough, though, we prepare for the worst. Like so many others, when Erica is stressed and busy, she stays up late working (cutting into sleep), struggles to get out for even a short walk, stress-eats empty carbs between meetings, and orders too much unhealthy takeout. We've seen this often enough that when we know an intense push is coming, we build in safeguards and contingency plans to protect her health from being hijacked by stress and lack of time. We also address the sources of her stress: specific circumstances related to her work, and work-related habits or tendencies that make things harder than they need to be.

Lack of sleep stimulates your appetite for unhealthy foods and inhibits your brain's ability to make good decisions. If you're sedentary on top of that, you'll feel even worse, since exercise helps so much to reduce feelings of stress. Exercise also promotes your brain's decision-making capacity. Finally, if you cope with stress by consuming high-carb, inflammatory processed foods, you'll increase feelings of brain fog and fatigue. None of these habits help you manage that stress, or perform well under high pressure. If anything, you'll spiral down. And if this all sounds too familiar, please don't feel ashamed or too judgmental about yourself. This response to stress and pressure is very common and even normal.

I've been someone who responds to stress and emotional upset by shoving my feelings down with food, for much of my life. Healing and managing this pattern in myself is where much of my expertise comes from.

Here are some of my best tips for breaking a pattern of stress-eating and emotional overeating.

1. Recognize, with compassion, that you're doing it.
People who stress-eat or get caught up in emotional eating get angry and frustrated with themselves. You may judge yourself as weak and berate yourself harshly when you've "done it again."

The next time you get an impulse to stress-eat junk food, or are in the middle of plowing through a bag of chips, slow down. Pause before you reach for the food, or put down what you're eating. Ask yourself: "What's wrong?" Allow yourself to feel what you're feeling. What is it?

You'll be surprised at the answer, sometimes. Maybe you're worried that you'll never get promoted. Maybe you're upset at yourself for not having good boundaries at work, and what that means for your personal well-being. Maybe you're experiencing—yet again—those anxious feelings about being an undeserving, soon-to-be-revealed impostor in your workplace.

Maybe you just haven't done anything fun or relaxing in a very long time, and this is the only way that you get to relax. So you deserve it, darn it! This last one is a pointer to the fact that you probably desperately need more relaxation and (non-destructive) fun in your life, however you can get it.

2. Learn and notice the difference between hunger and appetite.

When I'm craving something yummy, sweet, chocolaty, or salty, but want to cut down on emotional snacking, I'll ask myself this: "Would I eat an apple right now?" If the answer is no, that means I'm not hungry. And if I'm not hungry, something else is driving the craving. It's usually a restless kind of appetite, which means I'm bored, stressed, tired, or anxious.

Reconnect with your body and its signals. Try, as much as possible, to only eat when you're hungry, to eat mindfully, and to stop when you're reasonably satisfied (not stuffed). Get to know what hungry feels like. It's a very different feeling from the cravings of appetite.

If you'd like to decrease unnecessary snacking, and to stop using food as a way to deal with stress or feelings, keep going back to this question when the cravings come: "Am I actually hungry? (i.e., would I eat an apple, or something healthy, right now?) Or am I just craving some stimulation or comfort through food?"

I've found that it's much harder to go ahead with stress-eating, when I acknowledge to myself that that's what I'm doing. I'm more likely to choose something soothing but guilt-free instead, like some berries or a cozy herbal tea. Sure, I still have moments where I eat a bunch of cookies because I really want them, but that happens much less often than it used to.

*3. Find ways to calm, destress, or nourish yourself
that don't involve foods you'll regret.*
If I catch myself tempted to emotionally eat, I try to choose or do something healthy and life-giving. Something that addresses the distress that's driving the craving. Something that will truly make me feel better, versus binging on something that gives a temporary rush but leaves me feeling worse when it's over.

Maybe I'll go to my bedroom and journal, writing out my feelings or fears and then processing them on paper (usually I'll see that whatever it is, I've blown it way out of proportion, or I'll come up with good solutions). Sometimes I'll go out for a walk while listening to my favorite music, and blow off steam that way. Other times I'll find somewhere quiet to sit and pray. If I'm stressed, "praying" is usually more like venting—telling God all the details of my fears, worries, and frustrations, especially if they're things I don't feel I can admit to anyone else. I find that that really helps me.

4. Cultivate awareness of how different food choices make you feel.
I regularly encourage Erica, the high-octane executive, to pay close attention to the foods that increase energy and focus, and those that leave her tired and less effective. She has learned (because I asked her to pay attention and report back) that if she eats a lunch with a nutritious source of protein, with vegetables and minimal carbs, she feels alert and energized in her busy afternoons. The opposite happens if she eats a high-carb comfort-food meal. Notice how your food choices impact your energy and mood. This will help you make good decisions when you're under pressure and trying to decide what to eat.

I know from experience that when I'm moody and grumpy, alcohol and sugar are the last things I should choose, especially if I'm alone. It would be fun and dopamine-boosting in the moment, for sure. I'd feel better for a few minutes. But then my brain would feel more irritated and edgy, and my mood would plummet more. I'd probably get triggered and find it hard to stop eating. Alcohol increases my appetite along with cravings for sugary foods, salty foods, and carbs. The alcohol would also impact the quality of my sleep (the caffeine in the chocolate that I'd eat probably would, too), and I'd feel even worse the next day.

When I'm feeling moody and tempted to binge-snack, I try to keep myself busy. I look for something that will burn off negative energy and lift my spirits. I might find an instructional flamenco dance video online, move the living room table out of the way, and dance. One particularly rough night a few weeks ago, I felt much better after twenty minutes of this. I settled into a corner of the couch after, with a good book and a pile of fresh raspberries and strawberries. It's important to note that this type of snack hadn't seemed nearly as appealing when I was feeling irritated, blue, and like I needed to throw a "party" by myself.

Dancing in your living room might not be your thing at all. But what would be? I know there's something.

COACHING EXERCISE

Make a list of things that help you relieve stress and feel better.

Make these things that you genuinely enjoy, that are relatively easy to access in the moment, that you can do the next time you catch yourself wanting to stress-eat or stuff down emotions. They should be things that you won't feel regret about afterward.

Keep them in a notes app on your phone, or some other place where you can reference your list quickly when you need it (for example, in a moment when you're feeling upset and tempted to relieve your negative emotions through eating comfort foods).

5. Set yourself up for success.
Know your downfalls and triggers. What foods are you likely to reach for when stressed or bored, that you later regret? What foods, when you

start eating them, are almost impossible to stop eating? I recommend that you don't keep these trigger foods at home and don't have them close at hand at work, as a starting point.

What are the circumstances in which you'll be most likely to stress-eat or want to use food to avoid uncomfortable emotions? Be aware of what those are, and when they are happening (or are likely to happen). Have some contingency plans in place. Another client confessed to me that she always goes through the drive-thru at a fast-food restaurant and orders a burger and fries after a bad day at work. She still does this after stressful days, but she found a healthier type of takeout that she now gets as a reward and comfort.

Also, know what foods work for you and can serve as healthier substitutes in those moments when you feel too stressed or tired to go and *do* something other than eating. Popcorn is a trigger food for me. I'm incapable of stopping once I start, no matter how big the bag. So, I don't keep bags of popcorn at home. We just have popcorn kernels, which my husband pops for us on movie nights (the idea of hot oil and exploding little kernels makes me too nervous to make it for myself; this is probably a good thing). I've also discovered a yummy snack food made from snap peas that's high protein and high fiber and has low levels of carbs. It works for me in those moments when I'm craving a salty carb-like snack, and I can only eat so much of those at a time.

I love to relax by watching a show and snacking. That will probably never change. I try to have quick-access veggies in my fridge (precut carrots, cucumbers, celery, and those cute little tomatoes), and will often pair them with some kind of dip so that I have something to eat while watching. Something that tastes good but carries zero regret—and makes me healthier and smarter at the same time.

Coaching Exercise

Make a list of specific foods and situations that trigger you to stress-eat or overeat.

Next, for each of these, make a sample plan related to that trigger food.

How can you set yourself up for success and fewer regrets?

Are there certain foods you could simply stop buying or having around?

How about restaurants that you want to stop going to, or things you want to stop ordering?

Make a list of snacks or foods that comfort you, or that you enjoy, that you would consider to be healthier, less regret-provoking options.

What could you plan to do or eat the next time you find yourself in a particular stressful or emotional situation (based on your list of trigger situations)?

Notice, notice, notice. This is so key. When you cultivate awareness, it becomes much harder to engage in automatic habits or responses that you'll regret later.

When you choose foods that nourish your body and brain, you'll feel the difference. When you make food choices that don't truly support you, you'll notice how much worse you feel, if you're paying attention.

Eventually, this awareness of how different choices feel (and how they affect your performance, and even the way you look) starts to naturally drive those good choices. It becomes much easier to nourish yourself well. It becomes a way of life. And that, my friend, is a million times better than white-knuckling (and inevitably quitting) as you try to follow some rigid diet.

11

USE MOVEMENT TO BOOST YOUR BODY, MOOD, AND BRAIN

Yolanda, a newly minted lawyer, came to me for help. She had started working at a firm, and felt overwhelmed by the pace and workloads. More so, though, she felt overwhelmed by her thoughts and anxieties about work. She ruminated to the point of feeling paralyzed. Worse yet, these thoughts and anxieties would spill over into the little free time that she had. Her whole life felt awful.

Two things really helped her. First, we examined her most common and distressing thought patterns. She worried a lot that she would somehow fail or get fired. She kept thinking that she wasn't good enough for this career, and that she would end up destitute. That was all pretty easy to fix. She was obviously very bright, diligent, and conscientious. Her teachers, supervisors, and mentors had always appreciated and recognized her for doing good work. We kept talking about this until her anxious brain fully received that truth. She even made a notes file in her phone, of her list of "truths." If the thoughts started up again, she would remind herself of the truth (referring to her phone if necessary), and the noise in her head calmed down.

My second intervention dramatically improved her capacity to shake off stress. It physically empowered her brain to focus on more accurate, anxiety-calming thoughts. With my encouragement, Yolanda got back into running. Many of the high-achieving people I work with are former athletes, or used to be very active before work took over their lives. I use movement and exercise with every person I work with to help them counteract stress, boost their moods, and improve their cognitive and work performance.

Right away, Yolanda noticed how much a lunchtime run cleared her head and gave her the energy to power through the rest of her day. She also observed, as I had asked her to, that she felt noticeably worse on the days she didn't run. She'd feel more anxious, stressed, and tired, and was much more likely to feel overwhelmed. She could predictably improve her days, especially the worst ones, by exercising.

REGULAR EXERCISE AS A RESILIENCE STRATEGY

Researchers from the Department of Psychiatry and Behavioral Neuroscience at the University of Chicago examined the impact of regular exercise on emotional resilience.[1] They subjected participants who regularly exercised at least once a week to a social stress test, and compared their responses to those of people who didn't normally exercise. They found that the mood of the non-exercisers was more significantly negatively impacted by the stress. The exercisers were more likely to maintain a positive mood under stress, and also felt more "friendly" after the stress test (I love that). The researchers also noted that regular exercise was frequently associated with general well-being and lower rates of mood and anxiety disorders in cross-sectional studies. Keep in mind, too, that their baseline qualifier of exercising once a week really isn't much. But it's still enough to provide some protection against acute stress, apparently. Do whatever you can—every bit of exercise and movement helps.

USE MOVEMENT TO ENHANCE THE CAPACITY, PERFORMANCE, AND RESILIENCE OF YOUR BRAIN

A recent review paper, published in *Frontiers of Behavioral Neuroscience*, reported on the contribution of physical exercise to the resilience of the brain itself.[2] In the words of the authors, "exercise represents an important tool to influence neurodevelopment and shape the adult brain to react to life's challenges." They note that, among many other beneficial effects, exercise interventions have been associated with cognitive improvement and stress resilience in both humans and animals, and also seem to counteract the development of disease in the brain.

The authors also point out that "the beneficial influence of physical activity/exercise on resilience can in part by attributed to the understanding that it can induce positive physiological and psychological improvements, protect against the effects of stressful events, and prevent or minimize several neurological diseases." In adults, physical exercise has often been shown to slow cognitive decline, as well.

Some of my favorite neuroscience research, which gives me so much hope about aging well, demonstrates that exercise can physically enhance older brains. One of the most dreaded things about getting older, especially if you're a high performer, is worrying that your memory will start to go (or, worse, noticing that is already is). One such report, in the *British Journal of Sports Medicine*, examined the impact of twice-weekly aerobic training, for six months, in a group of women in their seventies who showed signs of mild cognitive impairment.[3] Follow-up MRI studies showed that those who had exercised aerobically increased the volume of the hippocampus, a structure that plays a key role in learning and memory. They concluded that "given the growing evidence that exercise is beneficial for cognitive and brain health, physical activity should be a standard recommendation for all older adults regardless of cognitive status."

Whether you're on the younger or older side of the age spectrum, your brain loves it when you move. It's not a coincidence that many of the world's most influential leaders have a disciplined, can't-miss daily exercise habit built into their lives.

A TOOL FOR BEATING BURNOUT

In 2013, a group of Swiss researchers pilot-tested a twelve-week exercise training program in a small group of men who scored high on a burnout inventory screening test.[4] They found that the exercise very significantly reduced overall perceived stress, as well as symptoms of burnout and depression. The latter was a notable finding, as burnout can be a risk factor for developing depression.

A couple of years later, another small study demonstrated that both cardiovascular and resistance exercise reduce symptoms of burnout, in different ways.[5] After four weeks of an exercise intervention, those who participated in cardiovascular exercise for thirty minutes, three times per week reported increased well-being, as well as decreased psychological stress, perceived stress, and emotional exhaustion. I love to point out that a decrease in "perceived" stress means that the stressors in your life don't necessarily have to change. Because of the positive impact of exercise on your brain, you can handle stress better and your life starts to feel less stressful, period.

A second group in that study did not do any cardio but instead completed a thirty-minute resistance training routine three times per week for four weeks. They also reported increased well-being and a reduction of perceived stress. Notably, this group was found to demonstrate an increased sense of personal accomplishment. As I mentioned earlier, a loss of confidence, evidenced by a decreased sense of personal accomplishment, is one of the three main signs that you are burning out. Strength training appears to counteract that. It makes sense. Have you ever spent some time weight training, and then strutted out of the gym, feeling taller, sexier, and more confident? I rest my case.

Researchers have yet to unequivocally confirm, through large-scale trials, the specific impact of exercise with respect to preventing or reducing burnout. Still, given all the other known benefits of physical activity, I continue to recommend it as a tool to prevent and treat burnout. You'll feel better, and you'll be stronger and more resilient.

BUILDING MOVEMENT INTO AN OVERSTUFFED, TOO-BUSY, I'M-TOO-TIRED LIFE

I'll say it again: I don't want anything in this book to add to your burdens. It's not supposed to make you feel like you're failing, or that you have to find even more time to do things in a life that already feels like there's no room to breathe.

With most of the things that I discuss or recommend, the exchange is in your favor. If you sleep more and better, everything will feel easier. You'll naturally be more efficient and productive. If you eat foods that truly nourish and support you, your brain will function better and you'll have more energy. Exercising reduces feelings of stress, increases your ability to handle stress, enhances your brain's performance, and increases your overall sense of well-being.

If you sleep better, eat better, and move more, it's unlikely that you'll feel more stressed and burdened. Quite the opposite, most likely. That said, it takes time to build in new habits, to figure out how and when to make the changes. It takes time and energy to identify healthy foods that you like and figure out how to fit them into your life. Shopping, cooking, ordering at restaurants, planning snacks; it's a lot to think about. And it's wise to tackle one habit change at a time instead of trying to change it all at once.

So, let's talk about specific ways you can build in more movement.

1. Pick something you like to do.
Some people discover, through consistent willpower and teeth-gritting discipline, that they no longer hate running. They may even come

to love it. This has never happened to me. I'm just not a runner (not that I've tried very hard to shift that position). I'm not saying that you shouldn't try running, if you've always wished you could be one of *them*. Still, I would argue that if your life is full of stress and distress, exercise shouldn't be another part of your life where you have to push, grind, and generally feel miserable.

Pick something that you like to do, to start. Is there a type of movement that you enjoy so much that time goes by easily, and you don't think of it as "exercise"? Walking and dancing do that for me. I've loved going for walks since I was a teenager, and I've been obsessed with dancing since I was a child. I would walk and dance even if there weren't any health benefits. I can dance and walk for hours under the right conditions (e.g., hiking a winding forest path with friends on a beautiful day, or dancing at a club that's playing fantastic music).

What types of movement did you love when you were younger? Were there exercise or dance classes you enjoyed taking? Team sports? Could you get involved with these again?

What sports or activities did you wish you could have done as a child? Could you try them now? A colleague of mine always wanted to take ballet classes as a child, but wasn't able to. A few years ago, she joined a gym and saw that they offered a barre class. She joined that class, and loves it. She told me that it feels like she's giving that little girl inside her the chance to live out her "ballet dream." Is there something like that in your life?

One of my clients really enjoys participating in group classes, rather than exercising alone. She's learned that if she signs up for scheduled classes (Pilates or HIIT/high-intensity interval training) at her local gym, she'll keep her promise to herself to work out regularly. If she's signed up, she'll go. When her gym was closed due to COVID-19 precautions, she pivoted to online classes, and this strategy still worked. As long as she'd prepaid for a class, she'd show up when the event came up on her calendar.

2. Choose activities that work with your schedule and your life.
Maybe you used to have a gym membership and loved going in the evenings after work, before you had kids. Your first inclination might be to sign up again, but think about your life first.

What do you feel most like doing? (See #1.) What time of day, or which specific days, would you be most likely to successfully do it?

Many of the professionals I work with find that tying their exercise to their work routine is helpful. Maybe your office has a gym that you can use. If you work from home, maybe you could invest in some home fitness equipment. Some of my clients use part of their lunch break, or use another break, to go for a walk or run. Maybe you can stop by the gym on the way home. That can help get your workout out of the way, especially if your entire household descends on you once you walk in your front door.

I work from home a lot of the time, and I either start or end my day with a power walk. I might also go for a walk in the middle of the day if I'm feeling tense, stressed, or foggy. I also throw in a bit of stretching or weights during strategic breaks. What would work for you? You can always get more sophisticated or scheduled once exercise becomes a feel-good, non-negotiable pillar of your life.

3. Keep it small and simple at first.
Start with something simple and easily achievable. Maybe it's a short walk or run, one day a week. Maybe it's a fifteen-minute YouTube workout in the morning, before the house wakes up. There's no need to set big goals right out of the gate. You want small wins—they'll motivate and encourage you. Haven't exercised in years? Add something simple in, one day a week, as a starting point. If your "plan" makes you feel overwhelmed, or makes you want to quit before you even start, you need to dial it back. You need to realistically be able to say, "Yeah, I *know* I can do this. No problem."

4. Rope other people in, if you can.

If you struggle to keep your promises to yourself, or know that you'll be tempted to skip it when the appointed moment arrives, get other people involved. Set up a walking date with a friend, or attend a regular fitness class together. I know people who make walking dates to talk and walk by phone or other communication apps with friends and loved ones who live far away. One of my friends goes mountain biking with her neighbor every Wednesday evening in the spring, summer, and fall; they switch to cross-country skiing in the winter.

One of my clients was struggling to find time to exercise after she got a big promotion. In the moment, work pressures always seemed more important than her plans to get out for a run or to a class. So, she hired a personal trainer who virtually works out with her twice a week. She finds it so helpful, that they still meet for their sessions even when she's vacationing on another continent.

Join a running club. Join a hiking club. Do whatever you can to be accountable to others, if it helps you get moving. Social support and community are so important to your well-being anyway, so it's a double win.

5. Don't expect to feel like doing it, when the moment comes.

I always warn people about this one. If exercise isn't a can't-miss habit yet, you'll be tired and want to skip it. The couch sings an irresistible siren song.

You'll say to yourself: "Today was a really tough day. Forget going for a walk; tomorrow would probably be better anyway."

No! Resist this! Get yourself out the door, or downstairs to your little workout area, or whatever it is you have to do. Do it, even for just a few minutes.

Next, notice how good you feel after. *This* feeling—the mental clarity, the stress relief, the elevated mood, the strut in your step—*this* is what will motivate you to keep your promise to yourself next time you're tired and the couch beckons again. One day, you'll arrive at the point when you feel stressed by the thought of missing your daily movement, because it makes every day so much better.

COACHING EXERCISE

Build a baseline plan to start moving more, by answering these simple questions.

- *What physical activity do you or would you enjoy that would be simple for you to start doing ASAP?*

- *When would this best fit into your schedule?*

- *How often do you think you can realistically do this, at least to start? And for how long at a time? (Make it easy—for example, a fifteen-minute walk three times a week after dinner.)*

- *What would you need to do to make it happen? (Pack gym clothes to work? Set up a workout area in your home? Get your partner to watch the kids? Sign up for a membership? Text a friend to set a date?)*

- *Is there someone you could be accountable to, to either encourage you in your plan or participate in the activity itself?*

PART VI

LIVE WITH MORE MEANING
AND PURPOSE

12

THE ART OF CRAFTING A
PURPOSEFUL LIFE

My friend's voice shook, and then the tears came. Her sobs made her sentences sound choppy and ragged. I'd never heard her so upset. And it wasn't because she had lost someone she loved, or had received terrible news.

She had read a book.

It was one of those books that insists that every person has an epic, soul-shaking, awe-inspiring purpose to their life. And that we must, at all costs, identify that purpose and then live it out. We must start that charitable foundation, invent that life-changing thing, rally our community around a cause, end poverty, write that best seller, be a world-changer, whatever it is. It's never anything "ordinary." And, according to books like the one she had read, if we miss that "capital *P*" purpose piece of our lives, we let down the world. Some imply that you fail at your life if you miss this. I imagine you know the kind of book, speech, coaching program, or inspirational video that I'm talking about. I even espoused similar ideas in my writing and speaking work in the past. I had read some of those books and listened to some of those gurus.

Of course, some people were born to do amazing things. Some people do have big callings. Our world *is* better because of many of them, and will be impacted by those yet to come. Maybe you're one of them. If so, know that I am cheering for you. But also know that I will still be cheering for you if you're just trying to make your tiny corner of the world a better place, through ways too small to ever make the news. Big or small, it all counts.

I love inspirational songs, movies, and stories. I love an inspiring motivational speech (if it aims high but still acknowledges most people's reality, rather than pushing magical thinking). I'll be the one who cries over a great narrative about someone who started out disadvantaged, who changed their part of the world, or relieved suffering somewhere.

But these days, I have an issue with anyone who carelessly insists, without considering the potential consequences, that everyone is called to do something *more*, something *bigger* than what they're already doing. That your own life, as it is, *isn't enough*. I've seen this preached from the stage at women's conferences, for example, and it really frustrates me.

My friend, the one who was crying, is an amazing woman. For years, she has worked full time, serving marginalized individuals in her community. She also has two young daughters, and is the kind of mom who makes professional-quality, whimsically decorated cake pops for her kids in her extremely limited free time. You should see the birthday parties she throws. She genuinely loves doing these things. She's marvelously creative and full of love.

That book, though, made her feel like she was failing. She cares deeply for others and the state of the world, and she worried that she wasn't doing enough. She also knew that she realistically could not do more with her life. Every minute was accounted for. There would be no *more* for her.

I realize that in telling this story, I run the risk of making my friend look superficial, excessively privileged, or just silly (someone who must not have any "real" problems), because she got so upset over what seems like a fluffy thing. But I know her. The book—and she probably only had time to read the first chapter—caught her in a moment of exhaustion, burnout, and vulnerability. She already gives so much to her clients and to her family, and so little to herself. The idea that her efforts weren't enough, that she needed to identify a greater calling and do more, at a time when she was already at her limit, tipped her into despair. It was so ironic—because to anyone who knows her, her life is profoundly purposeful already.

When I criticize these "rah-rah" calls to change the world, I'm thinking of the impact of a message like that on working parents who are stretched to their limits, or single moms who are working three jobs and trying to feed their kids. These people, and many others, are already champions. They are heroic. I see powerful purpose in their incredible, yet "ordinary" efforts. Heaven help someone who, in front of me, tries to tell these people that they need to do something big with their life. They already are.

WHAT DOES A PURPOSEFUL LIFE LOOK LIKE FOR YOU?

So, let's talk about you now. I encourage you to consider this final topic of purpose and meaning in life, from your unique perspective and context. Purpose comes in lots of different shapes and sizes. Our world tends to glamorize things that are big and flashy, without recognizing the immensely important contributions (and purposes) of the people who quietly, faithfully show up for their non-glamorous lives, day after day. This doesn't mean that such individuals don't dream of doing other things, or won't go on to do those things, but I believe it's so important to be able to find and connect to the purpose in your present circumstances. I know that it's there.

Think back to the exercise about your top four priorities from Chapter 3. What were they? I encourage you to look back at those right now, or to do the exercise if you haven't yet. One or more of those priorities, and possibly all of them, likely point to key sources of meaning and purpose in your life. Think about what those aspects of your life mean to you. Let that meaning sink in. Claim the purpose that you find there. Going forward, hold those things close to your heart. See those elements of your life as more deeply important than ever.

If you're not really feeling this, I have something else for you. Dr. Paul T. P. Wong, PhD, a Canadian clinical psychologist, researcher, and professor, created a research tool called the Personal Meaning Profile (PMP)[1] to measure people's perception of personal meaning in their lives. In his introduction to the questionnaire, he notes that a meaningful life typically involves a sense of purpose and personal significance. He also points out that "people often differ in what they value most," and have "different ideas as to what makes life worth living." This might mean that others don't understand what matters to you. That's okay—we're not all the same. Thank goodness! There's a marvelous saying I learned in Mexico: "Hay gente para todo," which means "there are people for everything." We have such varying roles in society, and society needs every one of us.

Dr. Wong's PMP consists of a series of fifty-seven statements that point to where an individual might derive their meaning in life. There are seven general categories that he has identified as sources of meaning for people:

- Achievement (e.g., "I engage in creative work")

- Relationship (e.g., "I relate well to others")

- Religion (e.g., "I believe that life has an ultimate purpose and meaning")

- Self-transcendence (e.g., "I strive to make this world a better place")

- Self-acceptance (e.g., "I accept my limitations")

- Intimacy (e.g., "I have a good family life")

- Fair treatment or perceived justice (e.g., "I am treated fairly by others")

If you, like many people I talk to, feel frustrated by a lack of purpose or meaning in your life, I encourage you to have a look at the questionnaire (it's easy to find online). It's intended to be used for research purposes, but simply looking at the sample statements and seeing which sources of meaning you score highest on may be useful to help you gain clarity on what matters most to you in life. The odds are high that it's in your life already.

WHY DO PURPOSE AND MEANING MATTER?

I've thought a lot about the topic of purpose for a couple of decades, and I've been delighted to see all kinds of interesting research emerge in this area. Here are some of the benefits of being connected to purpose and meaning in your life:

1. If your life feels meaningful, you feel better.
Dr. Michael Steger, PhD, is the founder and director of the Center for Meaning and Purpose at Colorado State University. According to Steger, having a sense of meaning in your life is correlated with experiencing a positive mood and positive emotions such as love, joy, vitality, curiosity, happiness, and hope.[2]

2. More meaning is associated with less depression, anxiety, and stress.
Steger also notes the established relationship between increased meaning and decreased depressive symptoms (and vice versa). High levels of meaning are also associated with less anxiety symptoms and lower levels of perceived stress.[2]

3. People who feel a strong sense of purpose are
more likely to choose healthy behaviors.
One compelling study found that people with a higher purpose can be more proactive in taking care of their health.[3] They were more likely to use preventive health care services, and each unit increase in purpose was associated with 17 percent fewer nights spent in the hospital.

4. Purpose and meaning can lengthen your life.
In 2019, researchers from the University of Michigan School of Public Health published a study that analyzed the association between life purpose and mortality.[4] Based on their analysis of data from a national cohort study of American adults over fifty years old, people without a strong life purpose were more than twice as likely to die earlier than those who had one. This surprising pattern was found consistently, independent of people's financial circumstances, gender, race, or education level. Sounds to me like an easy way to extend your life!

5. A sense of meaning can prevent burnout.
Polish health psychologist Dr. Dariusz Krok, PhD, illustrated this through a study that examined the protective relationships between meaning in life and burnout in firefighters. According to Krok, meaning may prevent or decrease the symptoms of burnout through "the fact that meaning in life enables individuals to interpret and organise their experience, identify important aspects of life, and achieve a sense of purpose and significance."[5] He found that firefighters with higher levels of personal meaning reported less emotional exhaustion and depersonalization (recall that these are the primary symptoms of burnout), and more personal accomplishment.

In a powerful statement, he shares that the results from his study imply that "individuals who experience meaning in life and pursue significant life goals in such domains as personal achievement and engagement, relationships with others, self-acceptance, and justice in the world are characterized by less feelings of being emotionally exhausted by one's work, impersonal and detached responses to various aspects of the job, and also by more feelings of personal accomplishment, competence, and efficiency at work."

This is wonderful news, no? I love that these aspects of life that give meaning, that are so beautiful and life-giving, literally give life to you, and your work. Even if your main sources of meaning don't come from your work. Your life can still be full of all kinds of meaningful purpose. And then you bring that full heart into your work, and into everything else you do.

MOVING FORWARD WITH PURPOSE, MEANING, AND RESILIENCE

You've made it to the end. Bravo! We've covered a lot of ground. I hope that it made you think a lot about your life.

After all the discussions around your health, work, stress reduction, mental health, life purpose, and more, what stands out to you?

COACHING EXERCISE

As usual, I've got some questions for you.

(If you haven't done so already, go get your Resilient Life Workbook at susan-biali.com/resilientworkbook, as you'll have space to write down the answers there; alternatively, use your journal or whatever works best for you.)

What do you love about your life?

What gives the most meaning and purpose to your life?

What do you want to change the most?

What do you want (or need) to get rid of?

What do you want (or need) to stop doing?

What do you want your life to be about, going forward?

When we're overly busy, as you probably are, it's natural to just focus on getting through the days and weeks. We can live that way for years, and steadily drift away from what matters most to us.

Sometimes, being powerfully and purposefully aligned with your work has a dangerous drift of its own. That happens to me. I'm so passionate about what I do that I can easily tip over into burnout or neglecting the people in my life (who also form a big part of my purpose). I have to really watch this, as it's a constant risk.

Take time to reflect on who you want to be in this world. How do you want to show up for your work, for the people in your life, for your community, and for the world? Again, it doesn't have to be in a big or fancy way.

I believe that I have several responsibilities. I have to do the work that I feel called to do. I love it, it has deep meaning for me, and it seems to make a difference to the lives of other people. I also have a responsibility to live in integrity with what I teach (and I need to live with integrity, period). I need to take care of myself. I need to live and work wisely, so that I avoid burnout and protect my mental health. I must prioritize people. I must do my best to embody love, not selfish ambition. I also need to share whatever prosperity I have with others, and not just hoard it for myself. These pieces and others, such as the importance of my faith, form my personal manifesto.

What forms yours?

By the way, it's easy to believe that it's too late to make changes. Sometimes things have been the same way for so long that it feels impossible to turn the ship around. Don't fall into that error. Take a good look at yourself and your life. It's not too late to shift your focus to what matters most, even if it's just in small increments. And remember to savor what's beautiful about your life already. I know that there's purpose and meaning there—you may just have lost sight of it.

Take care of yourself. Love people. Know what matters. Do what matters. In doing so, you will live a sustainable, satisfying life that has an impact.

COACHING EXERCISE

One more, before I go: A day in your ideal life.

Ten years from now, what would a day in your ideal life look like? Write out a one-page description, and have fun with it.

Describe the details of your day, from waking up in the morning to when you go to bed at night. What are the key elements of that ideal day? Imagine that anything is possible.

Here are some aspects to think about as you come up with that description:

Where are you living? Who do you live with? In what type of living space?

Who are your neighbors? Who are your friends? How are you engaged with your community?

What do you do in a typical day?

What gives your live meaning and purpose at this time?

What gives you the greatest joy?

What is your life about, if you could summarize it in one sentence?

Finally, what will you need to do in your life, from today forward, to increase the probability that this meaningful, purposeful future might come to fruition?

Is there one primary thing, or several? Write that one thing down, or make a list.

Now go do that.

Life is short. Live it well.

REFERENCES

INTRODUCTION

1. Ungar M. Change your world: the science of resilience and the true path to success. 2nd ed. Toronto (ON): Sutherland House; 2020.

2. American Psychological Association. Building your resilience [Internet]. Washington, DC: American Psychological Association; 2012 January [updated 2020 February]. Available from: https://www.apa.org/topics/resilience_

3. Epel ES. The geroscience agenda: Toxic stress, hormetic stress, and the rate of aging. Ageing Res Rev. 2020 Nov; 63:101167.

CHAPTER 1

1. Nobel Prize Outreach AB 2022. The Nobel Prize in Physiology or Medicine 2009 [Internet]. Stockholm, Sweden: The Nobel Foundation; 2022 February. Available from: https://www.nobelprize.org/prizes/medicine/2009/summary/

2. Benson H, Beary JF, Carol MP. The relaxation response. Psychiatry. 1974 Feb;37(1):37-46.

3. Benson H (Harvard Medical School, Boston, MA). The evidence-based emergent self-healing capacities of the relaxation response [Unpublished lecture notes]. Lecture for: The New Science of Resiliency and its Clinical Applications course (Harvard Medical School, Boston, MA). 2013 Sept 17 .

4. Bhasin MK, Dusek JA, Chang BH, Joseph MG, Denninger JW, Fricchione GL, Benson H, Libermann TA. Relaxation response induces temporal transcriptome changes in energy metabolism, insulin secretion and inflammatory pathways. PLoS One. 2013 May 1;8(5):e62817.

5. Ornish D, Lin J, Chan JM, Epel E, Kemp C, Weidner G, Marlin R, Frenda SJ, Magbanua MJM, Daubenmier J, Estay I, Hills NK, Chainani-Wu N, Carroll PR, Blackburn EH. Effect of comprehensive lifestyle changes on telomerase activity and telomere length in men with biopsy-proven low-risk prostate cancer: 5-year follow-up of a descriptive pilot study. Lancet Oncol. 2013 Oct;14(11):1112-1120.

6. Werner CM, Hecksteden A, Morsch A, Zundler J, Wegmann M, Kratzsch J, Thiery J, Hohl M, Bittenbring JT, Neumann F, Böhm M, Meyer T, Laufs U. Differential effects of endurance, interval, and resistance training on telomerase activity and telomere length in a randomized, controlled study. Eur Heart J. 2019 Jan 1;40(1):34-46.

7. Starkweather AR, Alhaeeri AA, Montpetit A, Brumelle J, Filler K, Montpetit M, Mohanraj L, Lyon DE, Jackson-Cook CK. An integrative review of factors associated with telomere length and implications for biobehavioral research. Nurs Res. 2014 Jan-Feb;63(1):36-50.

8. Ornish D (Preventive Medicine Research Institute, Sausalito, CA). The transformative power of lifestyle medicine [Unpublished lecture notes]. Lecture for: Lifestyle Medicine: Tools for Promoting Healthy Change 2018 (Harvard Medical School, Boston, MA). 2018 June 22.

9. Ornish D, Scherwitz LW, Billings JH, Brown SE, Gould KL, Merritt TA, Sparler S, Armstrong WT, Ports TA, Kirkeeide RL, Hogeboom C, Brand RJ. Intensive lifestyle changes for reversal of coronary heart disease. JAMA. 1998 Dec 16;280(23):2001-7.

10. Hölzel BK, Carmody J, Vangel M, Congleton C, Yerramsetti SM, Gard T, Lazar SW. Mindfulness practice leads to increases in regional brain gray matter density. Psychiatry Res. 2011 Jan 30;191(1):36-43.

11. Singleton O, Hölzel BK, Vangel M, Brach N, Carmody J, Lazar SW. Change in Brainstem Gray Matter Concentration Following a Mindfulness-Based Intervention is Correlated with Improvement in Psychological Well-Being. Front Hum Neurosci. 2014 Feb 18;8:33.

12. Van Dam NT, van Vugt MK, Vago DR, Schmalzl L, Saron CD, Olendzki A, Meissner T, Lazar SW, Kerr CE, Gorchov J, Fox KCR, Field BA, Britton WB, Brefczynski-Lewis JA, Meyer DE. Mind the Hype: A Critical Evaluation and Prescriptive Agenda for Research on Mindfulness and Meditation. Perspect Psychol Sci. 2018 Jan;13(1):36-61.

13. Dossett ML, Fricchione GL, Benson H. A New Era for Mind-Body Medicine. N Engl J Med. 2020 Apr 9;382(15):1390-1391.

14. Fricchione G (Harvard Medical School, Boston, MA). Mind Body Enhancement of Resiliency [Unpublished lecture notes]. Lecture for: The New Science of Resiliency and its Clinical Applications (Harvard Medical School, Boston, MA). 2013 Sept 17.

15. Ungar M. Change your world: the science of resilience and the true path to success. 2nd ed. Toronto (ON): Sutherland House; 2020.

16. Bellis MA, Hardcastle K, Ford K, Hughes K, Ashton K, Quigg Z, Butler N. Does continuous trusted adult support in childhood impart life-course resilience against adverse childhood experiences - a retrospective study on adult health-harming behaviours and mental well-being. BMC Psychiatry. 2017 Mar 23;17(1):110.

17. Denninger J (Harvard Medical School, Boston, MA). Relaxation Response: Mechanistic and Clinical Studies [Unpublished lecture notes]. Lecture for: The New Science of Resiliency and its Clinical Applications (Harvard Medical School, Boston, MA). 2013 Sept 18.

CHAPTER 2

1. World Health Organization. Burn-out an "occupational phenomenon": International Classification of Diseases [Internet]. Geneva, Switzerland: World Health Organization; 2019 May 28. Available from: https://www.who.int/mental_health/evidence/burn-out/en/

2. Freudenberger MA. Staff burnout. J Soc Issues. 1974 Winter; 30: 159–165.

3. Shanafelt TD, West CP, Sinsky C, Trockel M, Tutty M, Satele DV, Carlasare LE, Dyrbye LN. Changes in Burnout and Satisfaction With Work-Life Integration in Physicians and the General US Working Population Between 2011 and 2017. Mayo Clin Proc. 2019 Sep;94(9):1681-1694.

4. Deloitte Insights. Workplace Burnout Survey [Internet]. New York, NY: Deloitte; 2015. Available from: https://www2.deloitte.com/us/en/pages/about-deloitte/articles/burnout-survey.html

5. Threlkeld K. Employee Burnout Report: COVID-19's Impact and 3 Strategies to Curb It [Internet]. Austin, TX: Indeed for Employers; 2021 March 11. Available from: https://www.indeed.com/leadershiphub/preventing-employee-burnout-report

6. Peterson, AH. How millennials became the burnout generation [Internet]. New York City, NY: Buzzfeed News; 2019 Jan 5. Available from: https://www.buzzfeednews.com/article/annehelenpetersen/millennials-burnout-generation-debt-work

7. McKinsey & Company. Women in the Workplace 2021 [Internet]. New York, NY: McKinsey & Company; 2021 Sept 27. Available from: https://www.mckinsey.com/featured-insights/diversity-and-inclusion/women-in-the-workplace

8. The Lancet. Physician burnout: a global crisis. Lancet. 2019 Jul 13;394(10193):93.

9. Physician & Patient Surveys. The Physicians Foundation 2021 Physician Survey: COVID-19 Impact Edition: A Year Later [Internet]. Boston, MA: The Physicians Foundation; 2021 Aug 4. Available from: https://physiciansfoundation.org/physician-and-patient-surveys/the-physicians-foundation-2021-physician-survey/

10. Plieger, T. et al. Life stress as potential risk factor for depression and burnout. Burn Res. 2015 March; 2: 19-24.

11. Maslach C, Jackson SE. The measurement of experienced burnout. J Occ Behav. 1981; 2, 99–113.

12. Bianchi R, Schonfeld IS, Laurent E. Burnout-depression overlap: a review. Clin Psychol Rev. 2015 Mar;36:28-41.

13. Wurm W, Vogel K, Holl A, Ebner C, Bayer D, Mörkl S, Szilagyi IS, Hotter E, Kapfhammer HP, Hofmann P. Depression-Burnout Overlap in Physicians. PLoS One. 2016 Mar 1;11(3).

14. Leiter MP, Maslach C. Six areas of worklife: a model of the organizational context of burnout. J Health Hum Serv Adm. 1999 Spring;21(4):472-89.

15. Anchor S. Are the People Who Take Vacations the Ones Who Get Promoted [Internet]? Boston, MA: Harvard Business Review; 2015 June 12. Available from: https://hbr.org/2015/06/are-the-people-who-take-vacations-the-ones-who-get-promoted

16. Twaronite K. The Surprising Power of Simply Asking Coworkers How They're Doing [Internet]. Boston, MA: Harvard Business Review; 2019 Feb 28. Available from: https://hbr.org/2019/02/the-surprising-power-of-simply-asking-coworkers-how-theyre-doing

17. Swider B, Zimmerman R. Born to burnout: A meta-analytic path model of personality, job burnout, and work outcomes. J Vocat Behav. 2010; 76: 487-506.

18. Cross R et al. Collaborative Overload [Internet]. Boston, MA: Harvard Business Review; 2016 Jan-Feb issue. Available from: https:// hbr.org/2016/01/collaborative-overload

CHAPTER 3

1. Fricchione G (Harvard Medical School, Boston, MA). Mind Body Medicine: The Importance of Hormesis for Health [Unpublished lecture notes]. Lecture for: Herbert Benson, MD Course in Mind Body Medicine (Benson-Henry Institute for Mind Body Medicine at Massachusetts General Hospital, Boston, MA). 2021 Nov 3.

2. Epel ES. The geroscience agenda: Toxic stress, hormetic stress, and the rate of aging. Ageing Res Rev. 2020 Nov;63:101167.

3. Dhaval D, Kelly IR, Spasojevic J. The Effects of Retirement on Physical and Mental Health Outcomes. Southern Economic J. 2008;75(2):497-523.

4. Benson H (Harvard Medical School, Boston, MA). Stress management: Exploring the relaxation response [Unpublished lecture notes]. Lecture for: Lifestyle Medicine: Tools for Promoting Healthy Change (Harvard Medical School, Boston, MA). 2013 June 21.

5. Bhasin MK, Dusek JA, Chang BH, Joseph MG, Denninger JW, Fricchione GL, Benson H, Libermann TA. Relaxation response induces temporal transcriptome changes in energy metabolism, insulin secretion and inflammatory pathways. PLoS One. 2013 May 1;8(5):e62817.

6. MacCormick H. How Stress Affects Your Brain and How to Reverse It [Internet]. Stanford, CA: Stanford Medicine Scope 10K; 2020 Oct 7. Available from: https://scopeblog.stanford.edu/2020/10/07/how-stress-affects-your-brain-and-how-to-reverse-it/

7. Fox KC, Nijeboer S, Dixon ML, Floman JL, Ellamil M, Rumak SP, Sedlmeier P, Christoff K. Is meditation associated with altered brain structure? A systematic review and meta-analysis of morphometric neuroimaging in meditation practitioners. Neurosci Biobehav Rev. 2014 Jun;43:48-73.

8. Tang YY, Hölzel BK, Posner MI. The neuroscience of mindfulness meditation. Nat Rev Neurosci. 2015 Apr;16(4):213-25.

9. Davidson RJ, McEwen BS. Social influences on neuroplasticity: stress and interventions to promote well-being. Nat Neurosci. 2012 Apr 15;15(5):689-95.

10. Hölzel BK, Carmody J, Evans KC, Hoge EA, Dusek JA, Morgan L, Pitman RK, Lazar SW. Stress reduction correlates with structural changes in the amygdala. Soc Cogn Affect Neurosci. 2010 Mar;5(1):11-7.

11. Ding X, Tang YY, Tang R, Posner MI. Improving creativity performance by short-term meditation. Behav Brain Funct. 2014 Mar 19;10:9.

12. McKeown G. Essentialism: the disciplined pursuit of less. New York: Crown Publishing Group; 2014. 260 p.

CHAPTER 4

1. American Psychiatric Association. What Is Depression [Internet]? Washington, DC: American Psychiatric Association; 2020 Oct. Available from: https://www.psychiatry.org/patients-families/ depression/what-is-depression

2. Bilsker D, Gilbert M, Samra J. Antidepressant skills at work. Vancouver, BC: BC Mental Health and Addiction Services; 2007. 68 p.

3. Liu Y, Ozodiegwu ID, Yu Y, Hess R, Bie R. An association of health behaviors with depression and metabolic risks: Data from 2007 to 2014 U.S. National Health and Nutrition Examination Survey. J Affect Disord. 2017 Aug 1;217:190-196.

4. Meyer JD, Koltyn KF, Stegner AJ, Kim JS, Cook DB. Influence of Exercise Intensity for Improving Depressed Mood in Depression: A Dose-Response Study. Behav Ther. 2016 Jul;47(4):527-37.

5. Boden JM, Fergusson DM. Alcohol and depression. Addiction. 2011 May;106(5):906-14.

6. Seligman MEP. Flourish: a visionary new understanding of happiness and well-being. New York, NY: Free Press; 2011. 349 p.

CHAPTER 5

1. Bravata DM, Watts SA, Keefer AL, Madhusudhan DK, Taylor KT, Clark DM, Nelson RS, Cokley KO, Hagg HK. Prevalence, Predictors, and Treatment of Impostor Syndrome: a Systematic Review. J Gen Intern Med. 2020 Apr;35(4):1252-1275.

2. Johns Hopkins Medicine. Mental Health Disorder Statistics [Internet]. Baltimore, MD: Johns Hopkins Medicine. Available from: https://www.hopkinsmedicine.org/health/wellness-and-prevention/mental-health-disorder-statistics

3. Canadian Mental Health Association. Fast Facts About Mental Health and Mental Illness [Internet]. Toronto, ON: Canadian Mental Health Association. 2021 Jul 19. Available from: https://cmha.ca/brochure/fast-facts-about-mental-illness/

4. Psychiatry Online DSM Library. Trauma-and Stressor-related Disorders [Internet]. Washington, DC: American Psychiatric Association. Available from: https://dsm.psychiatryonline.org/doi/10.1176/appi.books.9780890425596.dsm07

5. Zoellner LA, Rothbaum BO, Feeny NC. PTSD not an anxiety disorder? DSM committee proposal turns back the hands of time. Depress Anxiety. 2011 Oct 3;28(10):853-6.

6. American Psychiatric Association. Diagnostic and statistical manual of mental disorders 5th edition. Washington, DC: American Psychiatric Assoc Pub; 2013. 991 p.

CHAPTER 6

1. Ungar M. Change your world: the science of resilience and the true path to success. 2nd ed. Toronto (ON): Sutherland House; 2020.

CHAPTER 7

1. Rath T, Harter J. Your Friends and Your Social Well-Being [Internet]. Washington, DC: Gallup Business Journal. Available from: https://news.gallup.com/businessjournal/127043/friends-social-wellbeing.aspx

2. Massachusetts General Hospital Psychiatry Research. Laboratory of Adult Development [Internet]. Boston, MA: Massachusetts General Hospital. Available from: https://www.massgeneral.org/psychiatry/research/laboratory-of-adult-development

3. Mineo L. Good Genes are Nice, but Joy is Better [Internet]. Boston, MA: The Harvard Gazette; 2017 Apr 11. Available from: https://news.harvard.edu/gazette/story/2017/04/over-nearly-80-years-harvard-study-has-been-showing-how-to-live-a-healthy-and-happy-life/

CHAPTER 8

1. Perlow LA, Porter JL. Making Time Off Predictable—and Required [Internet]. Boston, MA: Harvard Business Review; 2009 Oct. Available from: https://hbr.org/2009/10/making-time-off-predictable-and-required

2. Kossek EE. Managing Work-Life Boundaries in the Digital Age. Org Dyn. 2016 July-September; 45(3): 258-270.

CHAPTER 9

1. Ben Simon E, Rossi A, Harvey AG, Walker MP. Overanxious and underslept. Nat Hum Behav. 2020 Jan;4(1):100-110.

2. Harvey AG, Murray G, Chandler RA, Soehner A. Sleep disturbance as transdiagnostic: consideration of neurobiological mechanisms. Clin Psychol Rev. 2011 Mar;31(2):225-35.

3. Wagner U, Gais S, Haider H, Verleger R, Born J. Sleep inspires insight. Nature. 2004 Jan 22;427(6972):352-5.

4. Barnes CM, Watson NF. Why healthy sleep is good for business. Sleep Med Rev. 2019 Oct;47:112-118.

5. Hafner M, Stepanek M, Taylor J, Troxel WM, van Stolk C. Why Sleep Matters-The Economic Costs of Insufficient Sleep: A Cross-Country Comparative Analysis. Rand Health Q. 2017 Jan 1;6(4):11.

6. Harrison Y, Horne JA. One night of sleep loss impairs innovative thinking and flexible decision making. Organ Behav Hum Decis Process. 1999 May;78(2):128-45.

7. Gordon AM, Mendes WB, Prather AA. The social side of sleep: Elucidating the links between sleep and social processes. Curr Dir Psychol Sci. 2017 Oct;26(5):470-475.

8. Hyatt M. Self-Care as a Leadership Discipline [Internet]. Lead to Win Podcast. 2018 May 22. Available from: https://michaelhyatt.com/podcast-self-care-leadership-discipline/

9. Kaplan LM (Harvard Medical School, Boston, MA). Obesity and Metabolic Risk: Different Disorders, Different Treatments [Unpublished lecture notes]. Lecture for: Lifestyle Medicine: Tools for Promoting Healthy Change (Harvard Medical School, Boston, MA). 2018 June 23.

10. The Nutrition Source. Sleep [Internet]. Boston, MA: Harvard T.H. Chan School of Public Health. Available from: https://www.hsph.harvard.edu/nutritionsource/sleep/

11. Cooper CB, Neufeld EV, Dolezal BA, Martin JL. Sleep deprivation and obesity in adults: a brief narrative review. BMJ Open Sport Exerc Med. 2018 Oct 4;4(1):e000392.

12. Kim TW, Jeong JH, Hong SC. The impact of sleep and circadian disturbance on hormones and metabolism. Int J Endocrinol. 2015;2015:591729.

13. Perlow LA, Porter JL. Making Time Off Predictable—and Required [Internet]. Boston, MA: Harvard Business Review; 2009 Oct. Available from: https://hbr.org/2009/10/making-time-off-predictable-and-required

14. Zhou E. (Harvard Medical School, Boston, MA). Sleep Problems: The Most Effective Lifestyle Medicine Interventions [Unpublished lecture notes]. Lecture for: Lifestyle Medicine: Tools for Promoting Healthy Change (Harvard Medical School, Boston, MA). 2018 June 23.

15. American Psychiatric Association. Diagnostic and statistical manual of mental disorders 5th edition. Washington, DC: American Psychiatric Assoc Pub; 2013. 991 p.

16. Qaseem A, Kansagara D, Forciea MA, Cooke M, Denberg TD; Clinical Guidelines Committee of the American College of Physicians. Management of Chronic Insomnia Disorder in Adults: A Clinical Practice Guideline From the American College of Physicians. Ann Intern Med. 2016 Jul 19;165(2):125-33.

17. Chang AM, Aeschbach D, Duffy JF, Czeisler CA. Evening use of light-emitting eReaders negatively affects sleep, circadian timing, and next-morning alertness. Proc Natl Acad Sci U S A. 2015 Jan 27;112(4):1232-7.

CHAPTER 10

1. Heianza Y, Ma W, Huang T, Wang T, Zheng Y, Smith SR, Bray GA, Sacks FM, Qi L. Macronutrient Intake-Associated FGF21 Genotype Modifies Effects of Weight-Loss Diets on 2-Year Changes of Central Adiposity and Body Composition: The POUNDS Lost Trial. Diabetes Care. 2016 Nov;39(11):1909-1914.

2. Lassale C, Batty GD, Baghdadli A, Jacka F, Sánchez-Villegas A, Kivimäki M, Akbaraly T. Healthy dietary indices and risk of depressive outcomes: a systematic review and meta-analysis of observational studies. Mol Psychiatry. 2019 Jul;24(7):965-986.

3. Shivappa N, Steck SE, Hurley TG, Hussey JR, Hébert JR. Designing and developing a literature-derived, population-based dietary inflammatory index. Public Health Nutr. 2014 Aug;17(8):1689-96.

4. Marx W, Veronese N, Kelly JT, Smith L, Hockey M, Collins S, Trakman GL, Hoare E, Teasdale SB, Wade A, Lane M, Aslam H, Davis JA, O'Neil A, Shivappa N, Hebert JR, Blekkenhorst LC, Berk M, Segasby T, Jacka F. The Dietary Inflammatory Index and Human Health: An Umbrella Review of Meta-Analyses of Observational Studies. Adv Nutr. 2021 Oct 1;12(5):1681-1690.

5. Smith PJ, Blumenthal JA, Babyak MA, Craighead L, Welsh-Bohmer KA, Browndyke JN, Strauman TA, Sherwood A. Effects of the dietary approaches to stop hypertension diet, exercise, and caloric restriction on neurocognition in overweight adults with high blood pressure. Hypertension. 2010 Jun;55(6):1331-8.

6. Parrott M. Brain Health Food Guide [Internet]. North York, ON: Baycrest Health Sciences; 2017. Available from: https://www.baycrest.org/getattachment/0c3275c8-2419-4f12-ad71-a890d5f70265/Brain-Health-Food-Guide.aspx

7. Poulose SM, Miller MG, Shukitt-Hale B. Role of walnuts in maintaining brain health with age. J Nutr. 2014 Apr;144(4 Suppl):561S-566S.

CHAPTER 11

1. Childs E, de Wit H. Regular exercise is associated with emotional resilience to acute stress in healthy adults. Front Physiol. 2014 May 1;5:161.

2. Arida RM, Teixeira-Machado L. The Contribution of Physical Exercise to Brain Resilience. Front Behav Neurosci. 2021 Jan 20;14:626769.

3. ten Brinke LF, Bolandzadeh N, Nagamatsu LS, Hsu CL, Davis JC, Miran-Khan K, Liu-Ambrose T. Aerobic exercise increases hippocampal volume in older women with probable mild cognitive impairment: a 6-month randomised controlled trial. Br J Sports Med. 2015 Feb;49(4):248-54.

4. Gerber M, Brand S, Elliot C, Holsboer-Trachsler E, Pühse U, Beck J. Aerobic exercise training and burnout: a pilot study with male participants suffering from burnout. BMC Res Notes. 2013 Mar 4;6:78.

5. Bretland RJ, Thorsteinsson EB. Reducing workplace burnout: the relative benefits of cardiovascular and resistance exercise. PeerJ. 2015 Apr 9;3:e891.

CHAPTER 12

1. Wong, PTP. Personal Meaning Profile (PMP) [Internet]. Paul T.P. Wong; 1998. Available from: http://www.drpaulwong.com/wp-content/uploads/2018/03/Personal-Meaning-Profile-PMP-Wong-1998-Scale.pdf

2. Steger, MF. Meaning and Well-Being. In: Diener E, Oishi S, Tay L. Handbook of Well-Being. Salt Lake City, UT: DEF Publishers.

3. Kim ES, Strecher VJ, Ryff CD. Purpose in life and use of preventive health care services. Proc Natl Acad Sci U S A. 2014 Nov 18;111(46):16331-6.

4. Alimujiang A, Wiensch A, Boss J, Fleischer NL, Mondul AM, McLean K, Mukherjee B, Pearce CL. Association Between Life Purpose and Mortality Among US Adults Older Than 50 Years. JAMA Netw Open. 2019 May 3;2(5):e194270.

5. Krok D. Can Meaning Buffer Work Pressure? An Exploratory Study on Styles of Meaning in Life and Burnout in Firefighters. Arch Psychiatry Psychother. 2016; 1:31-42.